THE PATH TO COSMIC CONSCIOUSNESS

A journey through initiation to enlightenment in the Sacred Andean Tradition

Sally Rossiter

TESTIOMONIALS

"A provocative text for the path that is opening in the Andes!"
Prof JJ Hurtak ph.D, ph.D; founder and president of *The Academy for Future Science* and the author of over fifteen books, including commentaries on ancient mystical and gnostic texts such as the *Pistis Sophia*.

*

Sally's book provides fascinating insight into the Andean tradition. After reading this book you can't help but live your life more consciously with a profound awareness, respect and gratitude of Mother Nature and the power to heal and transform our lives.
Dina Cramer; author of Millenium Meditations, a corporate life coach.

*

I highly recommend this timely book. It is the work of a highly qualified master who truly lives and understands her mystical spiritual tradition.
Herbert Brauer, Wildlife Cameraman (National Geographic and Discovery), winner of multiple awards for the film *The Last Lioness*. He is a Kuraq Akulleq.

*

Humanity must come together and shake hands. There are greater events to come. We must stand together and stop the senseless witch hunts and meaningless wars. We are children of peace, of spring, of nature, of love... we must stop killing each other and shake hands like two pilgrims lost in the forest. The key is Mother Nature.
Credo Mutwa – Spiritual leader and author of many books including; Indaba, My Children and The Reptilian Agenda with David Icke.

Published by Graysonian Press +27 11 4311274
www.graysonian.compat@graysonian.com

Copyright © 2012 Sally Rossiter

All rights reserved under international copyright conventions. No part of this book may be reproduced, stored in a retrieval system, or transmitted in any form or by any means electronic, mechanical, photocopying, recorded or otherwise without written permission from Graysonian Press.

Whilst every care has been taken to check the accuracy of the information in this book, the publisher cannot be held responsible for any errors, omissions or originality.

Cover designed by Big Cat Printers

ISBN 978-0-9872816-0-9

 At an early age Sally realised she was Clairaudient (she could hear Spirit and beings talking to her) and over subsequent years evolved her other psychic senses. However, she did not engage with her clairaudience and it took illness and loss in her mid-twenties to bring her back to her higher senses. Sally trained in many healing modalities, reaching the level of Mastery in several. With time, using what she had learnt as a base, she evolved intuitive healing methods, her own unique form of channelling and various metaphysical methodologies.

But further spiritual evolution lay on another continent, in the heart of the Andes, South America, where fourteen years ago she commenced training with two Masters from the Andean Tradition. She has subsequently received and integrated the highest level of initiation available. She continues to host workshops and seminars for one of her original Masters, and is head of the Order of Inakri, Africa – the Spiritual lineage of her tradition. She is also head of a community of several hundred initiates in South Africa which grows annually.

In her private capacity Sally runs a highly successful practice, teaching her intuitive healing and balancing methods, speaking publicly to motivate individuals to seek their own truth. Sally's life is a dedication of service to awakening consciousness on our planet.

CONTENTS

DEDICATION 8

ACKNOWLEDGEMENTS 9

CHAPTER ONE 13

SHIFTING REALITY 13

CHAPTER TWO 22

THE EARTH 22

CHAPTER THREE - THE WATER 31

CHAPTER FOUR - THE AIR 39

CHAPTER FIVE - THE FIRE 48

CHAPTER SIX - CEREMONY & AYNI 56

CHAPTER SEVEN - THE COSMOGONY,
THE CREATOR, DUALITY & ASTROLOGY 68

CHAPTER EIGHT - INTUITION & COMMUNITY 85

CHAPTER NINE - THE SHADOW AND INITIATION 95

CHAPTER TEN - APUS & COCA 109

CHAPTER ELEVEN - BABA CREDO AND THE
AFRICAN TRADITIONS 120

CHAPTER TWELVE - DUALITIES 133

CHAPTER THIRTEEN - INTENTION, PRINCIPLES & THE CHAKANA 142

CHAPTER FOURTEEN - KURAQ AKULLAQ, MASTER OF THE COCA 159

CHAPTER FIFTEEN - PROPHECIES 174

CHAPTER SIXTEEN - THE FIFTH AND THE SIXTH ELEMENT 185

AFTERWORD 191

THE INCAS INCORPORATE THE ANDEAN TRADITION 193

GLOSSARY 201

DEDICATION

With humility I dedicate this book to my fellow human brothers and sisters, our evolution as a species and our future on our tolerant planet - Mother Earth.

May we be blessed with the consciousness to move forward in grace and Love.

ACKNOWLEDGEMENTS

With the guidance of *Ille Tecsi Wiracocha*, The One without name, with the dedication and love of my Andean Masters, in particular *Kamaq Wageag*, the support and acceptance by my family, my parents, the inspiration and unconditional love of my son Gabriel, *Ulanga, Kanchay Amachaque*, and the generosity of spirit and kindness of my friends in the community of the *Order of Inkari* in Africa, this book and these experiences have come to pass.

My gratitude abounds.

Much gratitude and love to Donna Vance, Alto Misayoq of the order of Inkari, for the design and art work of the Chakana diagrams.

PROLOGUE

As Humans we are and always will be searching for the truth of our own reality, and everything around it. Through this searching and investigating in the micro - and macrocosm, we arrived at the threshold of the present millennium.

The immediate question arrives; what are we looking for? What reality do we want to experience? Is it not a new understanding of the physical, emotional, mental or spiritual realities?

Through this search for truth, a series of tools and methodologies evolved which are slowly improving and expanding our sensory organs and capacities. If we value this search for the truth, as explored by many cultures - inevitably we arrive at and must acknowledge extrasensory perception. Ultimately all cultures through history have imprinted on this path a sense of the magical, mythical, religious, philosophical, esoteric, mystical, and spiritual and multi-dimensionality which brings us to two diverging paths which in reality are the same; Science and Faith.

From my earliest years I have been an innate searcher of the existential truth and as such, studied innumerable disciplines in esoteric, philosophical, spiritual and mystic orders and have attained in these schools and traditions the highest level of initiation. It is with deep satisfaction, humility, clarity and ubiquity that I can say these disciplines have encountered their own truth, irrefutably, and when we bring together all these truths we find the ultimate truth.

It is at this juncture I encountered the "Sacred Andean Tradition", preserved and transmitted by the *Aumatas* - high priests of the Empire of *Tawantinsuyo,* four corners of the Inkan empire of the South American continent.

Within the teachings of the Sacred Andean Tradition there is a sense of our existence, evolving and interacting with the structural-energetic make-up of all that is. All manifested life has a structural and unique energetic vibration and clear purpose interacting with the other structures, co-existing in ongoing manifested evolution.

The basic principle of this Tradition is equilibrium, the harmony existing on Earth on which all the different structures are connected and are interacting permanently. Humanity is the caretaker of this natural equilibrium. Humans and the Earth have the same natural structure, except that humans have emotions. These emotions are the result of water and fire elements within the human makeup, and can be unstable.

It is with great hope that I perceive in the author of this book, an *Aumata*, high priest of the Andean Tradition, someone providing continuity to the concepts, perspectives and teachings. She, after many years of learning and assimilating with her natural and innate gifts, vision and intuition has provided a clear message of the truth of this Tradition.

Later in the book, the author expresses with clarity and understanding what the purpose of our existence is and more shows us how to continue in the Andean way, with sensibility, humility and truth, through balance of heart and logical reasoning.

This book truly addresses the theme with a sense of magic, spirit, mysticism and legend of the ancestral truth transmitted jealously from teacher to student for thousands of years. 'The Path to Cosmic Consciousness' is *khuya* (ours). It supports the sacred journey of the author and her persistent search through many years for the path of the Truth, Light and Unconditional Love.

Dr. Regis Llerena Paredes

Kamaq Wageaq

Kuraq Akulleq

The Order of Inkari

CHAPTER ONE

SHIFTING REALITY

At some point in this mystifying experience I become aware of my body. It was uncomfortable. It was itchy. The rocks and stones were hard and unyielding and I felt as though an ant colony was using me as a direct route to somewhere else. I couldn't stay in that position. Gingerly I turned myself over, aware of the silence around me, of others deeply absorbed in their experience. The Masters administered energy moving amongst the attendees, who all lay face down.

I glanced up at the sky and froze, my mind stunned into stillness. Above me, visible with my naked eyes, as clear and as real as the stones and grass around me, was an enormous vortex, a Mandala. It stretched I gauged, about 100 metres in diameter. It was high but directly above us, symmetrical and made up of soft hues – pink, lavender, yellow, blue white, orange and green. It was perfectly circular and reminded me of a lotus flower containing geometric patterns like petals. It breathed, contracting and expanding gently and rhythmically.

I thought I was hallucinating. The absurd thought crossed my mind - perhaps I had consumed cactus juice without noticing. I looked back at the ground, then at everyone else. I looked back up. It was still there. I rubbed my eyes, blinked and tried again. It was still there. Incredible. I wanted to shout out loud for everyone to look but I remained still, gazing upwards. My mind wanted rational explanations. There was no cloud directly above us. The sky was clear, and besides, the Mandala was transparent not opaque as it would have been if formed by clouds, I reasoned.

It remained with us for 10 minutes, maybe more and then slowly gently pulled apart and disappeared.

I did not talk immediately about what I had seen. I couldn't. Later that night we sat around a fire-circle, and I finally got it out, feeling uncomfortable in the following silence. However, there was another who had seen it, with the courage to confirm the vision; a lady called Nicole mentioned a few details that I had not, confirming the experience. Many years later I met Nicole again and she reminded me of what we had both seen that day. I cannot explain it nor can I forget it…

Fourteen years ago, I was not in a good place in my life. Within two weeks my reality shattered. My mentor who was a part of me from the age of 13, passed on from a prolonged Cancer. He had prepared me for so many aspects of life but ironically not his own death. The sheer shock of the experience threw me into my own illness in the form of Chronic Fatigue Syndrome. Then, I discovered that my long term relationship was at an end.

With what energy remained available to me I tried very hard to salvage pieces of my life but my levels of depression and exhaustion took over and I was rendered almost helpless. At that time there was little understanding of M.E. (Chronic Fatigue Syndrome). My Doctor offered vitamins as a solution! For those who have no experience of Chronic Fatigue, let me simply say that leaving bed, showering and dressing would sap my vitality entirely, and bed would beckon again.

Any extra activity performed in a day was through sheer will and determination. I realised I was on my own, in all respects.

Alternative energy healing methods, in particular Reiki, were recommended. This led me to my first Reiki workshop and although for many weeks I had no sense of this energy, I worked diligently on myself just hoping it would help. It certainly did. Within about six months I had not only developed a good sense of the energy but felt stronger. And so very gradually my healing began.

Over the next three years I managed to complete my Reiki training, further my studies of various other natural therapies and opened my own practice, and best of all I was still standing. It took many years for my heart to heal from the loss of my mentor, and even though I realized as my awareness changed, it had been a disempowering relationship, I loved him then and still do.

It was around this time my Reiki Master, Valentine Reineke suggested I attend a workshop being hosted by a client of hers, introducing to South Africa two South American Shamanic Masters. I knew very little about Shamanism and had a vague perception of men wearing animal skins, drinking suspect plant substances in remote parts of the world. However, I should also mention I had been actively healing myself for a number of years taking responsibility for my own wellbeing and happiness, But I had a deep sense of dissatisfaction and restlessness as though I had not found exactly what I sought.

I was a little wary by then, having exposed myself to many teachings, techniques and hundreds of New Age and Spiritual books. None led to a specific direction in my journey. I had brought healing to my body and my heart, but it required incredible effort on my part. I had had some amazing experiences and learnt the art of meditation but still I was unfulfilled and asked myself "What is missing?"

I agreed to attend this workshop, more to support Valentine's client whom I had never met, than because I had a burning interest in these matters.

On the day of the workshop which ran over three and a half days, I arrived early and waited outside the reception for registration to commence. There was a small group gathered and a short time later the organiser arrived with two men. Very ordinary they seemed to me, dressed like regular people and certainly nothing astounding. I must admit I felt more than a little disappointed. Where were the animal skins, bones and drums? I still wasn't convinced that I shouldn't sneak off and head home to spend the weekend lounging.

Sometime later the workshop started. The two Masters did not speak English, thus all conversation was translated from Spanish. Explaining the tradition, they told us it isn't a religion but a spiritual path. They were exposed to the Andean tradition more than thirty years prior, and had been drawn again to it after studying in various "mystery schools" and spiritual traditions. The simplicity and purity of the tradition drew them back. The reflection of nature, at the heart of the Andean tradition and its natural laws, are the same laws that govern the entire universe.

This was followed by a question and answer session. I sat near the back, feeling my bored facial expression and attitude were justified. A lady up front asked how she could better protect herself from evil. I do not believe in evil in the conventional sense and was irritated when the one master, *Kamaq Wageaq,* his name in Quechua, answered her with some practical techniques. My attention was drawn suddenly though when he said "... but, always but....if evil exists at a certain level and your perception is above that level you will see through evil, see it for what it is". I started feeling that perhaps I had not wasted my time after all, so I relaxed prepared to open myself a fraction to new possibilities and experiences.

Then a meditation was conducted, a visualisation into the Solar system. It was lovely and I particularly enjoyed playing on the rings of Saturn. Afterwards we had a break and as I left the conference room, *Kamaq Wageaq,* the master who had answered questions earlier, was at my side. He communicated to me that he too found Saturn to be an especially beautiful planet. I smiled and agreed. As I continued walking it hit me, how in Heavens name had he seen into my meditation? And how had he communicated with me when he spoke no English and me no Spanish? I was intrigued.

The following day we travelled to the Suikerbosrand Nature Reserve to conduct 'Earth practices'. The second Master's name is *Hatun Runa* and he spoke a little English and had us lie on the grass and with rocks on our stomachs; we made little holes in the grass, cupping our hands over them. Into these holes we talked to the *Pachamama,* 'Mother

Earth'. We could unburden ourselves, particularly telling her things relating to our physical world. That day I thought I had exhausted *Pachamamas'* listening skills. At our own pace we turned our heads, placing our ears over the hole and listening. I did as the Masters' directed, not knowing what to expect. Suddenly I heard a sweet rich voice inside of myself. "*Pachamama* speaks"!

Pachamama told me many things that day but what I remember most clearly were her words about the Masters, "They are my disciples. They travel the Earth teaching people of me and of my love for my people." I was stunned, but knew these simple words to be true.

The next day we worked with the water and the air elements. For the first time I was able to see the living energy of the air element. These are the Sylphs, the elementals living within air, nourishing it. I am certain that most people see them and simply dismiss their perception. I saw them as tiny transparent white molecules floating and bouncing around in the air. They are seen with the naked eye in soft light. That day I did not perceive the Earth elementals, the gnomes and elves, nor would I for many years.

On the final day we worked with the fire element. These experiences were energetically so powerful that I retained little conscious memory of them. It was as though, after the extraordinary experiences of the first day, my memory simply folded in on itself. I have experienced this subsequently, and then in meditation or at a later time when I can understand things at a pace acceptable to my human consciousness, I recall these experiences. This work with the four elements changed my perception of life.

One other significant thing happened that weekend although at the time I was unaware of its importance. *Kamaq Wageaq* again communicated with me, I thought in English but I could not be certain, saying the lady who had organised the workshop would be moving away in a year and asked if I would be prepared to help organise workshops in South Africa in the future. I responded, "Sure, no problem".

I assumed we spoke of arranging the type of workshop I was attending, about 30 people for a weekend. Little did I know my flippant response would commit me in the future to growing the largest non-indigenous shamanic community in South Africa, spanning several cities and encompassing hundreds of initiates. Was I in for a surprise.

The day following the workshop I eagerly undertook the first level initiation in the path of the Andean tradition. It is a one-day initiation and hosted out-doors in nature. The detail of the initiation process is sacred and as such is not something to be written here. With respect, I can say it brings a massive re-awakening of consciousness, taking months to integrate and I felt my life became an aligned reflection of my soul's journey after that initiation.

A minor but challenging personal issue healed for me in this initiation; my relationship with sugar. Since childhood I loved sweets, chocolates and sugar. I had to have a chocolate daily and thankfully my mother relented for the sake of her sanity. This continued into adulthood. When I received my Reiki Master attunement, years earlier my Reiki Master, Valentine, mentioned my relationship with sugar would heal when my relationship with my mother healed. This confused me as I have an excellent relationship with my mother.

In first level initiation I received clarity. I experienced a past life where the woman who was to birth me, unknown to me in this life, resisted me from conception. More than once she tried to induce a miscarriage, unsuccessfully. This memory and the sense of being welcomed and wanted by my current life family healed my addiction to sugar with no effort. Today my body does not tolerate chocolate.

During this initiation we received the beginning of our *Messa*. A Messa is a folded cloth, tied up with a thin cord. It consists of Llama wool fabric, folded in a certain way to hold objects of power. These objects can be personal, but generally are objects from nature, stones. When we take a stone, from places of significance we create a route of access to the power of that place. A stone from a Peruvian mountain connects me to the energy of that mountain and I can draw on it for use in ceremony or healing. Through the Messa we access immense power from all over the planet, used in the service of humanity and for the greater good. At this point in the Andean path, my understanding of the Messa was that it's a connection to and a manifestation of power - spiritual, energetic power.

We were instructed to take a stone from our place of initiation, and also how to take the stone. First, we looked for one that attracted us and then we asked permission to remove the stone from its home. If we didn't receive permission then we looked for another stone. Under no circumstances were we simply to take things from nature without requesting permission, whether a stone or a flower.

I recall returning home that night feeling more alive than I have ever felt in my life, aware, awakened and totally present. At the time I didn't fully understand the elements and their enormous power to heal us, their intimate relationship with our own inner nature, nor did I understand that a conscious relationship with them had been initiated within me.

The next ten months saw extraordinary change within me, and my life. My healing work was the only area that remained untouched by change. This area had been literally forced into change by my own physical illness in the preceding years. The forced change had resulted in moving from working in corporate environments to becoming a healer, and now required only growth, and it arrived in abundance.

My personal relationship which had been sorely compromised and neglected, left my life and with it my financial security. I changed residences. These were the external obvious changes but the internal ones were far more powerful and prolific, making the external possible. Over years I had stagnated, become bored and boring. I experienced life as dull and endured it. My 'joie de vivre' was non-existent, my fire dormant. There was security and routine but little else. And I was terrified of stepping out of that comfort zone. That first initiation made possible the clarity to admit I needed to change, the courage to change, and the faith to see me through. I clung to Spirit for my support and security. As a result my relationship with The Creator became a more real, and personal connection. My intuitive communication with Spirit grew and held fast. At last I was beginning to know myself, truthfully.

There was much clearing and healing before I could clearly express who I was becoming at the inner essence of my own being, but it was possible.

CHAPTER TWO

THE EARTH

"It was the first day of the workshop when the Earth practices were performed. We, the participants, were outside on the lawn. It had been explained that we should lie down on our stomachs, with our chins resting on our hands, and with our fingers make a small hole in the grass over which we could place our mouths. We could whisper to Mother Earth all our secrets, problems and challenges. We could tell her everything we were afraid or ashamed of and she would accept this from us. That done we were to turn our heads so that our ears rested over the holes we had made, and listen to what the Earth had to say to us.

I found a good spot under a tree and proceeded. I was telling the Earth all my problems when the thought struck me that I looked ridiculous. I had always felt that people found me strange, and here I was confirming their assumptions by talking to grass. At that moment a leaf fell from the tree directly onto the arch of my foot and simultaneously I heard this sweet, gentle, female voice "But I am listening…"

I began to cry and found I couldn't stop. I wept and wept and after some time realised there was movement around me. People were stirring. I tried to regain my composure but only succeeded in weeping more.

Finally I stopped and sat up to find all these people silently sitting waiting for me. I felt mortified, until Kamaq Wageaq asked me gently, "Are you feeling better."- Mabel

"I had been through years of pain and by the time I went on the Andean workshop I was ship wrecked, emotionally battered and bruised. My sister is an initiate in the tradition and literally nagged me to go with her. I had no expectation.

I lay on the lawn and made a little hole in the grass to talk to the Earth. The sun shone down on me. I told the Earth all my 'stuff' and I started to cry – it was easy to talk to the ground and just let things out, things I could not say to people, not even my family. I cried for a long time.

I heard a voice in my head, very distinctly saying that there will be a new heart. I didn't know what it meant but I felt better.

Since that workshop I am no longer an emotional wreck, my heart is more at peace. I have regained my sense of self and I can say that I am a happy person. My circumstances are still the same but I now make the best of them. At the age of forty-seven I have started a career, which is flourishing. With the help of a doctors' supervision I am losing weight, it is taking effort but it is happening.

I don't really understand the tradition or what happened to me, and I don't think I will initiate into it but I would certainly repeat the workshop." - Susan

By the end of that year the masters returned to South Africa to teach and offer the next level of initiation. I awaited their arrival with excitement and a sense of expectation. I was not disappointed.

The workshop was a beautiful affair, where again the attendants were introduced to the four elements. I was able to absorb more information from the wisdom and infinite knowledge the masters displayed, as opposed to the first workshop where I was in the experience with little recollection of the teachings themselves.

We again started with the Earth element. I have come to love the Earth deeply, or the *Pachamama* as she is known in the Andean Tradition. *Pachamama* is the manifestation of all that exists, it is nature. *Allpa Mama* is the Earth element itself and *Pachamama* is the matrix of the cosmos, it is the womb of material existence. It transforms all biological material into fertilizer and healthy materials for the Earth. The physical Earth is huge but her energetic manifestations are even greater, for example, when the Earths energies move or change there are powerful earthquakes and tsunamis. Their effects can be truly devastating.

We are not separate to the Earth; we are an extension of her. All the minerals, elements and vitamins produced by the Earth are contained in our bodies. When we are in our mothers' wombs, through our mothers' food consumption and her body, our bodies are formed from the Earths elements. At the end of our physical lives, when our bodies die, we return to the Earth and the cycle is completed.

Like a loving mother, she gives freely, asking only to be acknowledged for who she is and held with love. This is not an open-ended invitation for abuse because when we love, abuse plays no part. We want to support, care for, hold and heal. Through loving the Earth, respect becomes a natural quality of that relationship. Destroying her is no longer an option.

Many years after this workshop, I was invited to perform a ritual for a potential mining project in Zimbabwe. Two gents invited me, one involved in geotechnical drilling, the other a geologist. They were concerned for the damage that would be caused to the environment in a project of this nature. They also wanted permission from the Earth and the co-operation of the elements. I was nervous as I was uncertain how *Pachamama* would react to having huge holes blasted into her. I did rituals to honour the Earth and was amazed. *Pachamama* spoke and sent a message to her sons, "They can take what they want from me, it is theirs to take. I only ask that I am honoured."

Our beloved *Pachamama* is a living being and yet is often incorrectly perceived as simply a huge chunk of rock. She has consciousness but because she vibrates at a steady and slow frequency she is perceived as being solid and not living. She not only lives, she is the mother, the one who holds and supports us on our paths and journeys. She also provides us with our abundance. So often I come across people who ask Spirit or heaven to assist them with their financial, material issues but this is the long way round. It is the Earth who produces our food, supports our footsteps through life, provides our shelter, responding to and affected by our physical actions.

Pachamama has always been considered the reflection of the Heavens; she is the matter in which all Creation is moulded. As the feminine mother she is a symbol of fertility and also holds the key to our creative energies and abilities.

Each element resonates with a quality within us and the quality relating to the Earth is desire, or wanting. It is the desire to change, to create and to experience. The energy of our Will, our determination is held within this element. Through our relationship with the Earth we are endowed with better decision-making faculties and the capacity for action. Our day to day living is enhanced by this and so is our evolution as individuals, and as a species. Making healthy empowered decisions means making decisions based in love not fear; the love of ourselves, of our planet, our species and our Creator; without which the finality of Union with The Creator is thwarted. This union, in the Andean Tradition is the purpose of our existence and the ultimate fulfilment of each individual.

In our day to day reality the balance between the four elements within us and the qualities associated with these elements is vital. Without a balanced amount of 'Earth Energy' our will is weakened and we lack direction. We become ungrounded, unstable and unfocused.

The Andean Tradition recognises energy centres in the human body called *Nawis* - or eyes of energy. There are five *Nawis*, our lower energy centre is in direct contact with the Earth, and eye of energy is dark in colour and dense in vibration. It is the creative centre, giving life to our children. And it is through this centre that we are able to 'communicate' with the Earth element, which happens through the common elements, the minerals, which we share with her. This also enables better control over our latent energies, which exist in this centre.

When we work consistently with the Earth element, acknowledging our entire physical makeup exists because of the Earth, and we are a part of her, we become strong willed, constant and able to persevere. We will become stable, like trees well rooted into the

Earth. If we are well rooted, we are able to grow upwards towards our creator, as far as our level of consciousness allows us. Our tolerance levels grow and we become cautious, not fearful. We access consideration, patience, and the desire to be of service to others, to give of ourselves selflessly for the greater good. Our flow of give and receive is balanced and open, whatever we receive we return abundantly, like the Earth.

When a seed is sown, a plant grows from this seed and, in time, is able to return that seed multiplied many times over. The Earth element is very generous with us, her children.

Energetically the main function of the Earth Element is transformation. The Earth, because she vibrates at such a slow frequency, feeds on heavy vibrations. She absorbs our heaviness and transforms it into lighter vibrations. This symbolises the principle of infinite evolution, the process of constant change and the transmutation from heavy to light frequency, the process from unconsciousness to consciousness, journeying from fear to an open hearted state of unity. Understanding the Earth in this way is extraordinary and having access to her transformative abilities at our finger tips is a powerful tool for change, growth, development and balance.

By working with this element, one begins to understand the sacrifices that she symbolizes through her relationship to all manifestation are expressions of strength and power. Humans are matter, and subjected to 'attachment', but by becoming one with the Earth, we learn from her, the value of detachment, renunciation, which generates a stress free way of living. We become healthier and more prosperous when we engage with life for the sake of living. This means that we discard our fear of not having enough, we stop hording and taking excess from the Earth in out attempts to feel more secure.

Working with the elements increases our understanding of the *elementals*. These are the beings or specks of consciousness dwelling within the element and are the guardians of that element. They are intelligent manifestations of the Earth and plant kingdom with a unique expression. They have become the focus of legends and fantasy but, as a form of consciousness, are very real. Within and upon the Earth dwell the gnomes, fairies and green spirits. They are guardians of flowers, plants, trees, herbs, crystals and stones. They protect nature and solve all the small problems, which concern our beloved *Pachamama*. They hide from our human mind, able to dash into folds of space to escape our sensory vision.

Trees are a lighter vibration than the Earth, but still a part of her, like the skin that covers our flesh. They are as vital to her as they are to us, without them we would have to find artificial ways of producing oxygen or perish. Trees have an individualised consciousness, but are also connected into all other trees on the planet, primarily those of their own type. Trees are a manifestation of the Earth, but are connected into both the Earth and Air elements, existing both underground and above ground simultaneously.

Rocks are also a powerful manifestation of the Earth, in existence for millions and millions of years. In that time they have been exposed to wind, sun and rain and absorbed the consciousness of all they have witnessed. Through the rocks we communicate with our ancestors. Using time and consciousness we can tap into their infinite information regarding the evolution of our planet, her inhabitants and history as it unfolded. This is not as recent history has been recorded by individuals, through personal perceptions, beliefs and ideas which tainted events in specific ways.

Kamaq Wageaq told us that to harmonise a home we can take stones that we are drawn to, from nature, (with permission) placing them in the corners of the doors and windows.

He also told a beautiful story to emphasise the power of the stones still to be found in nature.

There were two stones - sisters. The one was a simple brown stone, without sheen or pretty markings and the other a beautiful piece of black obsidian, with depth and rich reflections. One day a man came to the mountain and laid his eyes on the obsidian, picked her up, deciding that she belonged in the temple. The obsidian was happy leaving the mountain and was placed in an honorary position on the altar in full view. For many years this sister took pleasure being admired and touched by the priests. But eventually she began longing for her home, her sheen dulling, her light dimming; she became a bored, unhappy stone.

Her sister on the other hand had had a wonderful time, absorbing the rays of the sun and communing with the earth. One day a great storm came, flashing lightning, creating a small river from the top of the mountain flowing into the valley. The little brown stone was washed away, tumbling and dancing as she went. Over years she made her way downwards, eventually flowing with the water into a greater river. She witnessed moon cycles, seasonal changes, stars in the sky, spoke with the wind, and was tickled by the water. She was in constant contact with the elements.

We must ask ourselves which stone has greater power, greater wisdom, which has witnessed more and has greater connection to the cosmos?

We are drawn to pretty stones with fascinating forms and beautiful colours but truthfully the plain stones in nature are the ones that have power because of their constant connection to the elements. Don't dismiss them.

Hatun Runa gave this beautiful prayer to the Pachamama, which I would like to share with you. In his own words. Thus in the same way that Master Jesus delivered to us the Prayer 'Our Father', also of Essene origin, he gave a Prayer for the Earth: 'Our Earth', the *'Pachamama'*, which was uncovered in the scrolls of the Dead Sea, near Qumran just a few years ago.

Oh Mother Earth, you that have given me birth and all the elements that constitute my body, receive my gratitude.

I plead that you remove the accumulated impurities, in order to transform them in thy laboratories.

Return them transmuted in the purest elements to help me accomplish my function and mission in this world.

Nojan Kani Pachamama - Meaning 'I am the Mother Earth'.

Our beloved Pachamama is strong and will outlive us all. While we are alive we are the caretakers of the Earth. To accomplish this, our consciousness, our love and respect for her are necessary. We are the children of the Earth and we need to care for our Mother.

CHAPTER THREE

THE WATER

"We were told to sit in the river on a rock but I didn't want to. I felt resistance. One of the Alto Misayoqs (third level initiate), Heather, saw me vacillating and gently led me into the river where she found the perfect rock for me. So I sat but still I felt resistance. Kamaq Wageaq approached me, wading through the water and bending forward he took the sun hat off my head. He cupped his hand, taking water from the river, and poured it over my head. He put my cap back on and walked away. I couldn't believe it but I started crying again. Suddenly my resistance vanished and I heard the gentle words of the water telling me to simply let it flow." - Sylvia

The second element presented at this workshop was water, the magic elixir required by all life. The Andean expression for water is *'Unu Mama'*, which is from the Quechua language meaning the first mother because water is the primary element within us. As the teaching began I listened, fascinated at what the Masters had to say about *Unu Mama*;

Water covers seventy percent of the Earth's surface. Scientists theorise that oceans formed upon the Earth's crust through a combination of liquid and gas released from inside the planet and the impact on the Earth of ice-laden comets from the heavens. Whatever the source of water, there are now six hundred million cubic kilometres of it splashing upon the Earth's crust, reaching a depth of eleven thousand meters in the Pacific Marinas Trench, where the pressure from the weight is equal to over a thousand atmospheres.

Oceans are separated into barren and fertile zones just like land. Massive rivers within the ocean, called currents carry water around the globe in huge circling patterns, influencing and influenced by global weather systems. Currents move quickly only at the surface, the deeper colder waters take about one thousand years to re-circulate to the ocean surface. With the remarkable exception of the ocean floor, where perhaps millions of species of life remain undiscovered, the depths' of the ocean are a desert compared with the dazzling garden of life inhabiting the more temperate, shallow zones. The upper two percent of the ocean's volume contains most biological organisms, at least those familiar to us. The ocean supports a greater diversity of living body types than land. The tree of life grows swiftly in water.

Water is essential for life as it is the origin of all life on our planet. Due to its properties, this marvellous element is the perfect medium for the growth of all living cells. All life emanated and evolved from water – inspired by the Creators' breath. Human beings are in fact simply big bags of water.

Water is greatly adaptable, with enormous neutralising powers. It adapts itself to the shape of the vessel into which it is poured. It even takes the shape of the human body. Water, in its liquid form, is always horizontal. The horizon over the sea, lakes, and all bodies of water always hold a horizontal surface even when the vessel in which it is contained is not level. Water is always in balance.

To go deeper into the symbolism of water; it is recorded that many Spiritual Masters are associated with water, and it is used in many religious ceremonies; Jesus walked on the waters, Moses was saved from the waters and he parted the Red Sea to lead his people to the Promised Land, Naranyana signifies the Spirit of God that floats on water and Baptism is performed with Holy Water. Practically for water to wash and purify us internally, it is necessary to establish a relationship with the spirit of water, the cosmic water.

All this factual information suddenly took on a new light as I viewed water as a living element, taking into consideration my own relationship with it, which had been an unconscious relationship.

Water is the feminine passive element, and she resonates with the moon, so healing practices or ceremonies performed with water are directly influenced by the moon phase at that point. As the moon grows so the power of the water element increases, as the moon wanes the power of the water is diminished.

Water is associated very strongly with our sentimental feelings, and when used consciously, she frees, cleanses and enables them to flow just as she does. It is because we, as human beings, contain so much fluid that we have such strong, frequent emotional reactions. Our minds lean to rational response but our feelings do not. Our internal water reacts to our feelings, just as the external physical element of water reacts to temperature. Our inner water can become like ice, when we block and harden our feelings. We hurt ourselves when we block our feelings in this way. When we become angered, reaching boiling point, it can be compared to our internal water being heated by our internal fire. These waters boil and then simply evaporate like steam. If we work consciously with water we are able to manage our emotional intelligence.

Water is the original cleanser, not only of our physical bodies and physical matter but also of all energies. When we shower or bathe we cleanse the denser energies in our energy field. When we meditate whilst sitting in water we activate our sentimental side, and can consciously release feelings and emotions. For 'airy' or 'fiery' people water is often very attractive. Subconsciously they are counter balancing the excessive air or fire elements in their psyche.

Like the sea, where so many forms of life are dependent on water, so we too have many different expressions of emotion. Above the surface of the ocean, where water interacts with other elements there are storms, tsunamis and hurricanes, so we too externalise powerful emotional reactions as we interact with life and the other elements.

Through water we develop our intuition, reflecting the upper world, the realms of Spirit. As the surface of a lake reflects surrounding mountains, so the element of water within us reflects our sixth sense, our cognitive intuition. In my healing work, I have found myself working more and more with psychic energy, in many forms including channelling and intuition. While working with psychic energy I am always thirsty and drink copious quantities of water. Psychic energy connects into and moves through the water element within us.

When we work with water we connect to beings, consciousness, residing in water as Nymphs, Tritons, Mer People and Sirens. They enable us to overcome tension, anguish, fear, anxiety, sadness, lack of affection, and we grow in patience, tolerance and serenity. I learnt on that initial workshop that these elementals reside in all water forms (rivers, lakes and oceans) and also in our blood, tears and internal systems.

Silence is the quality associated with the element of water. Its physical expression is to be without noise, to not talk. This silence enables us to go inward, become reflective and connect with ourselves, becoming more aware of our thought processes. There is also the state of inner silence, where the mind is resting. Thought ceases and our inner waters, our feelings become like the surface of a still lake. In this state we are open to listening, listening with our physical ears and our consciousness and tuning inwards to the silence. In this state of being we connect clearly to our intuition and ourselves. It is in this silence that all is created.

When we submerge ourselves in water, there are no sounds and it is akin to being in the womb of our mother, surrounded by amniotic fluids.

Through the submergence of self into our internal waters we are able to access our subconscious. In the depths of the ocean where there is neither light nor sound, through erosion, rain and tides, millions of years of planetary evolution are deposited. Within our subconscious the impressions of hundreds of thousands of years of human evolution exist. As we move beyond our conscious minds, deeper into our subconscious selves, we can access this unlimited well of information.

I have noticed in myself that when I am lacking water in my psyche, physically dehydrating, my mind becomes hyper active. I become scattered and my sleep patterns disturbed, often lying in bed unable to switch off. A lack of water creates an imbalance with air. At these times my digestive and urinary systems are affected and their functions disturbed. A lack of water also wreaks havoc with my body temperature, leaving me feeling the enormous heat generated by my internal fire. I also experience intense anger and even adopt an aggressive attitude. As soon as I hydrate myself I feel clearly the drop in body temperature, whilst an improved mood follows shortly after.

"Most people would agree to noticing when it rains or is overcast their mood or disposition can change, but this seems as far as most peoples' perception goes. I had a very clear experience of how the elements affect us.

We were filming 'Lion' in Africa. I had a new assistant on the trip who had great difficulty expressing himself. His ability to communicate was impaired and having exhausted all usual methods, I decided to try something a little unorthodox. The weather was strange with strong wind for days. It felt right ignoring the man, so for three days I did not address him directly and for three days the winds raged.

Mid-morning on the third day it began raining and at our lunch break, it suddenly felt right to talk to him. I confronted him directly on his inability to communicate. Things suddenly erupted in him emotionally and he was in tears. I did not back down but held the space for him to vent. When he was done I simply offered him tea. It seems as though, even though air governs communication, it was the element of water which needed to be addressed and balanced in him for his communication to flow. The man is now able to express himself well and we address each other in friendship." - Herbert

Some of the symptoms of excessive water in a person's psyche will result in excess emotion, with high levels of externalized sensitivity with blame being placed - in other words, being constantly aware of the slights and hurts inflicted on us but remaining insensitive to the feelings of others.

"Through realising that the elements live within us, as well as outside in our environments, I have become aware of the reflective state that exists for me between the internal and external elements. Recognizing them as a living consciousness has made

me aware of small significant signs in my relationship with the elements in my garden. For example; as I care for the elements outside, they show me things about my internal elements, when my garden needs water I usually do too; when the trees and shrubs are un-groomed, I am usually in need of self nurturing." - Mabel

Our bodily fluids move through many different systems within us. The liver is an area of emotional aggression in the body, which includes the fire element. In our lower abdominal area we hold our fears, worries and anxieties, in our hearts there is more graciousness, harmony and love. The emotional and evolutionary aspects of our nature affect the lymphatic system and reproductive glands. All these areas are affected by water, and various expressions of this diverse element can be directly associated with these organs and systems in our bodies.

The imbalance of water is responsible for all wars and conflicts on our planet. Liquids move the world. In the past there are examples of emotional battles, like the war of Troy and today wars are still motivated by liquids, like oil.

Kamaq Wageaq explained that the simplest way to connect with water and to experience her flow is to get wet. When it rains most people, like cats, run for cover. He suggested that the next time we are near a storm, we should go outside into the rain, feel it on our faces and our bodies, and allow the waters of the heavens to clean us energetically, to bless us.

"I was flying back from Lima, Peru having completed my third level initiation. What triggered it I don't know but my back went into spasm and shortly thereafter my legs were totally numb. I arrived back in South Africa in agony. I had a few hours before I

left for Zambia. I spoke with a friend who is also a high level initiate in the Andean Tradition who suggested I take a twenty minute shower, spraying the water onto the area in pain, and to focus on clearing it. When I stepped out of the shower twenty minutes later, the pain, stiffness and numbness was totally gone.

A few months later another new assistant joined us in camp, a very nervous chap. The conditions in the African bush aggravated his disposition and he developed a terrible rash. The rash started on his lower back and over several days crept up his back covering the areas over his kidneys. We had no medication on hand and medical care was days away. When I looked at the rashes pattern I realised it had begun in the Earth area of his body and had moved up into the water area. I suggested he lie down on the Earth, consciously releasing all his worries into the Earth, and he then should take a 'conscious' shower, using the water to release.

He performed these practices that afternoon and afterwards said that he had felt as though he was 'melting into the Earth' when he lay on the ground. By the next morning the rash was gone and his disposition greatly improved. Even though I have personally experienced the power of the elements I was amazed at the effect it had on someone who was inexperienced in element practices and who, under different circumstances, would never have tried what I suggested." - Herbert

CHAPTER FOUR

THE AIR

"The proceedings started with the smudging of our energy (incense being run through the energy field). *Meeting Kamaq Wageaq, and hearing of the work we would all do together over the next few days, I was struck by the dynamic power of this wonderful, openhearted Peruvian man. When he introduced us to the various elements I found I could understand them simply and easily.*

The tree and air exercises were very powerful for me. The trees reminded me of a time when I was a young child, a time spent with the trees held and protected by them, a time I had forgotten.

My experience with the air felt the same. When I was about six years old, the wind helped me to fly – if I ran fast enough, it would lift me up so I could pretend to be a bird flying above the ground, free. I again experienced that same innocent, pure connection." - Carol

"My Experience with the air was unexpected. Feeling the air flowing through me as I stood in the wind, I felt all the tensions drain out of my mind and thoughts. My mind let go and relaxed. As it happened I felt my heart expand and love flow from me." - Sylvia

On the third day as we filed into the auditorium, there was the sound of bells and chimes and incense billowed around us. In the Andean tradition a very special herb is burnt called *Wirajoya*. It is burnt with hot coals and over this, ground-up frankincense is sprinkled. The smell is quite wonderful and once you have been exposed to these teachings, that smell seems to reconnect you. *Wirajoya* is a herb grown in parts of South America, similar to *Impepo*, a herb used widely by *Sangomas* in South Africa. Both herbs are used for clearing - allowing energy to flow freely.

It quickly became obvious it was the day of the air, the subtle element we breathe and constantly process through our bodies. Air is the element of purification and relates to our mental bodies.

Simon, the translator who dedicatedly recited all that the masters said in Spanish into English, played the Didgeridoo very well. On the Air day he gave each participant a blast from his *Didge* over the Heart Centre. I felt the powerful vibration move through my body and my heart centre stirred as if nudged.

Kamaq Wageaq said that in order to connect with the elements, to communicate with them we cannot use the 'wrong' language, a verbal language. He said we must use the language of codes or keys, which enable access to the frequency of the elements and their vibrations. There are so many types of energetic codes or keys of access – genetic, sound, social, biological, DNA and energetic codes are a few. In the Andean Tradition we use sound, smell and a number of other tools to change the frequency, to encode new vibrations within the consciousness of a person. They are the keys that open the doors to other states of consciousness. You experienced the Didgeridoo when you came in, and this is a way of enabling you access to a different code, a different frequency which will make possible better communication with the elements, in this case the air.

As air governs communication, it is appropriate to mention this now. The air purifies whatever it connects with. This wonderful element channels energy in every way and in every direction, strengthening our lives and nourishing all of life and the Earth.

The air in Quechua is *Wayrachiy* and the wind in Quechua is called *Wayra,* air in movement. *Wayra* strengthens trees and plants, it can be a refreshing breeze and also it brings back gossip, chatter and knowledge of others and bygone times as well as problems and news from other places. It is the element of all communication. The wind brings this to us through human communication but when we learn to listen to the wind, it tells us these things directly.

Sylphs, Elves and Cloud Spirits are the elementals who support creation by purifying, blending, balancing, harmonising and controlling air which is critical to life on Earth. They are also the guardians of the elements energy. This core element is bound to human mental and intellectual skills and its elementals help us overcome our intellectual trials, guide our intelligence, convey the understanding of theories, enhance our mental and intellectual clarity, capitalise on our intelligence and set our intellect to the service of our total being.

The air elementals also balance our brain hemispheres. Air translates into pure energy in us and is a subtle element reflecting our entire mental state. When we align with it, our insight and thinking is clearer, we exercise more humility, tolerance and kindness towards those blindly unconsciousness.

When blended with blood (water element) air purifies, extending our physical lives (thereby helping the earth element) and together with fire (temperature), air thrusts us forward enhancing our awareness.

The air, through its elemental beings, creates wind, hurricanes, and refreshing breezes and the wind inspires tidal waves. They symbolise the shuddering, jolting motion that human beings undergo when their consciousness expands, like a butterfly breaking free of a limiting cocoon allowing their nature to blossom. Once freed the butterfly catches the wind in its wings and begins to fly, just as air brings higher understanding and consciousness to humans.

Kamaq Wageaq shared his experience of a Tornado in Wyoming in the United States.

I was driving a big camper, listening to music, chatting with my brother and the wind was blowing gently outside. All of a sudden the sky went dark, the wind stopped and there was total calm. Nothing moved. I stopped the car, got out and realised not even leaves stirred, there were no birds or bird sounds. It was a strange silence. We continued driving and then we heard an eerie sound... there was a tornado directly approaching us.

It was huge, maybe 400 metres across the horizon. I started to pray to *Ille Tecsi Wiracocha*, there was nothing else to do. Suddenly the Tornado changed direction, leaving us to contend with its outer movement, which pushed our heavy vehicle like a leaf, across the road and into a ditch. The power was enormous. Things flew all around us. And then as suddenly as it began it was over. We continued driving and finally reached a gas station. The people there asked us, "What are you doing here? Don't you know there is a Tornado in the area? There have been warnings on the radio." We had not heard any warnings because we were listening to music. The energy and the strength of the air is truly amazing.

I felt excited when after the lectures, we went outside to experience the air practices. The one in particular which I want to share is 'seeing the energy of air' (in other traditions this is also called *Prana*). *Prana* is vital life force, which exists in air and feeds our vitality. In gentle light, when we stare at a blue sky we see these small round 'cells' bumping and floating. When we did the practice I realised I had seen them many times before but had not recognised them. I believe it is the same for many people, who put it down to eyesight, fluff in their eyes or any number of rational explanations.

I observed the movement of these tiny cells as they floated towards a tree. I could see an 'aura' around the tree, which looked like a mirage created by heat. It was about five centimetres wide all the way around the tree. As I watched, these little cells bumped against the trees aura and floated away or where absorbed into the aura. I realised I was seeing the tree absorbing oxygen from the air, literally being fed by this element. *(this is my experience – Sally)*

Air purifies and energises us, we cannot live without oxygen and we cannot live without *Prana*.

This element has helped me to clean up my mind and thought process. For all of us, a mind that is in chaos creates a reality of chaos. When we think a certain way our emotions and our bodies follow the attitude of those thoughts and react accordingly.

The quality associated with air is knowledge and it certainly governs communication. The deeper experience is knowledge that has become wisdom and deeper forms of communication, for example telepathy and channelling.

Most of us confuse thought and mind, when in essence thought is interference in the true state of our minds. A purified mind is clear and open, like a blue sky without clouds. It is a state of mental peace. In this space our intuition flows freely. We often hear about 'being present', or living in the present. When our minds are still, from thought, and our consciousness is directed into our current experience (the moment) we are able to experience presence of being and this is simply described as being present. It is an authentic experience of living life in fullness and we are alert to the currents flowing through our lives. There are no surprises. Intentions set in this mind state manifest quickly, undisturbed and unhindered by our doubts and our mental noise. It is akin to planting seeds in fertile soil.

Air enables us to communicate telepathically with other humans, with the plant and animal realms and with other dimensions of Spirit. By the second workshop I was made deeply aware of the power of air in this non-physical expression as telepathy.

At this stage I assisted a little with the organisation of the workshop. The following year the role of organiser would fall to me, and other initiates who were able to help.

One of my chores that year was to go into town on the day of the first level initiation, collect supplies that were needed, and return to the mountains with them. The workshop organiser had dropped the masters and the initiates at a sacred mountain and had gone on to arrange other practicalities for the days to follow. She must have been delayed, because the masters and the initiates were left on the mountain in African heat in midsummer without refreshments.

Driving back towards the mountains, I heard *Kamaq Wageag's* voice asking me to bring fruit and water for everyone. I hesitated, but decided to stop and buy it anyway. At worst I would be stuck with a lot of extra fruit. On arrival at the mountain I found some very parched people who greeted me thankfully. *Kamaq Wageag* did not comment, he simply said *'Gracias'* like it was the most normal experience.

The second experience occurred erasing all doubts. The same year the masters hosted a separate healing class after our Andean Workshop. I had some healing experience and they allowed me to work on one of the patients being helped that day. Afterwards I was approached by *Kamaq Wageaq* with an instruction regarding my healing. I did not understand what he was telling me (the Spanish - English problem) and asked one of the ladies who is fluent in Spanish, to help me. I asked *Kamaq Wageaq* to repeat to her what he wanted to tell me. He did so but the advice still did not make sense to me. He must have read it from my facial expression. In the next moment I heard his voice as clear as if he had spoken out loud but in my mind, saying, "Do not doubt me, I tell you the truth". I was stunned and stared at him agape. He gave me a stern look and walked away.

I soon became accustomed to this form of communication with him. In fact I found it very comforting and it was certainly practical. I also learnt a lot. I found I could ask questions and he lovingly and patiently gave me information. This communication was not limited to him being physically present and has been a constant from that point forward. I have never found this communication invasive nor has it diminished my own capacity to manage and control my mind. To the contrary, it has helped me to understand the limitlessness of my mind; it sharpened the skill of my consciousness and enabled me to communicate with all life forms in this way.

I had, from the first workshop, communicated with the Earth and had had some good conversations with trees, and now something interesting began to happen. I found that if I projected my awareness to anything living, my frequency would adjust to facilitate communication. In my work and my daily living, opportunities began to manifest where I could practice this. In this way I was able to communicate telepathically with animals. I found horses and cats the easiest to access. I loved chatting with dogs but found their response a little slower than cats and horses. It seemed to take them longer to realise what was happening. On one special occasion I communicated very successfully with the birds in my garden. Unfortunately the clarity of that first communication has never been repeated, and although I can still access bird consciousness it is not in the same way.

Over the years and the continual experience of my consciousness I have naturally accessed some incredible phenomena. And truthfully, these are amazing experiences', they remain however simply phenomena. At first these things astounded me, now they are ordinary and simply an expression of whom and what I am. The real goal lies beyond phenomena; it is the ultimate union with *Ille Tecsi Wiracocha*, the state of oneness with nature and the Divine. Phenomena are really tools to help us on that journey; they bring guidance, information and help as mind and consciousness expand. Alone without the ultimate journey, they are empty toys.

Air also plays a huge role in our process of creation. We have a thought (air) which, following its mental conception, is put into action to become a manifestation. Through the air we are able to access possibilities, ideas of what can be, and through a combination of water (silence), fire (daring) and Earth (desiring) that manifestation takes place.

We can forgo eating for quite some time, or stay thirsty for a shorter period of time, but try to endure just a few minutes without breathing air.

"I stood between the rocks high up above the valley in what is called 'the wind tunnel'. As I climbed up to reach this place I felt my consciousness ascending to a different state. And now looking down over the valley, I felt the wind blow away my immediate past, taking my hurts and transforming me deep in my cells. And then I looked down at a scene from another time, in a moment of great peace for me.

Beneath me lay the plains of another country, in another time and I knew I had died in battle, lying on the ground and no longer hearing the screams of human suffering but the gentle whispers of the wind as I left this world.

The time and place changed before my eyes and I saw myself walking on the Moors of Scotland, observing the landscape and feeling the wind caressing my skin.

Again the scene changed. This time I was looking onto the lands that spread below me but in another time. I saw myself as a male, dressed in traditional Peruvian clothing. I felt that I was a warrior in training. I had lived and died on these lands. I had been happy here. The images faded and I felt the words forming in my mind, "six hundred years ago". I knew somehow that this was the time when the reality of the last vision had taken place.

I have remained connected to the wind ever since then. It calms me completely. When the wind blows, I take myself out doors and immediately enter into a deeply peaceful state of contemplation." - Marlene- Ollyantaitambo, Peru

CHAPTER FIVE

THE FIRE

"I was deep in meditation. Kamaq Wageag was guiding us through an internal experience of the four elements within our own bodies. Prior to this I had been feeling grumpy, irritated and physically uncomfortable. I felt resistance to being in this meditation.

When we reached fire my body became increasingly hot. I felt I would pass out if it continued. I was burning from the inside. I wanted to open my eyes, but realised that my consciousness was in another dimension. My intuition urged me to keep my eyes closed. I felt the urgent need to lie down on the tiled floor for relief. Again my intuition urged me not to, but rather to lean forward in my seat to attract Kamaq Wageags' attention. Within moments I felt my body temperature stabilizing.

I no longer felt any resistance, I was happy to go with the process and let things flow. Later I understood that anger and irritation are 'heavy' or 'shadow' aspects of fire, and experienced when our fire is unbalanced." - Mabel

On the final day of the workshop we rose before dawn and gathered at the base of a small hill for the *Inti Raymi* ceremony. *Inti Raymi* is the celebration of the first rays of the sun; these light rays are received with joy and celebration. So we were equipped with items of festivity made up of candles representing the colours of the rainbow, incense burners, a bell, and the Cuzco flag - also the colours of the rainbow, wine, fruit and beautiful pipe music. During the ceremony the rays are received through our heart centres and move through our upper energy centres, enlightening and bestowing understanding on us...

Watching the sun lighting its path over the horizon that morning, I was struck by the beauty and harmony of the process. All of nature came alive to welcome the sun and a new day was born. We made offering of wine and fruit to the sun, celebrating its arrival, just as the birds, trees and insects were doing.

In many towns in Peru, especially Cuzco, the *Inti Raymi* ceremony is performed on the Winter Solstice (Southern Hemisphere). Many years later I attended this celebration in *Saccsaywaman*, which is a citadel made from gigantic rocks, situated above the town of Cuzco. It was a re-enactment by actors dressed in glittering finery of the Inka court, including representation of the Inka and the Q'olla (female counterpart to the Inka), nobility, priests and Aumatas. Several thousand tourists and locals attended this festivity of dance and celebration.

It was a spectacular sight, especially when several hundred warriors came running over the crest of the hills brandishing the Cuzco flag. But truthfully, I did not experience the harmony and connection felt that day watching the sun rise, and which still expands my heart with every sun rise ceremony I witness.

"I had experienced an underlying sadness for a long time. So many events had transpired over years that it was hard to recognise the origin. I was aware of the sadness that morning. Standing on the hill I realised I didn't need to open my eyes to see the sun's first rays, I felt them. My heart chakra expanded hugely and I cried gently from the sweetness of it all. I felt this overwhelming love and I knew, in that moment that we are all loved, all of humanity, all of life. I saw mental images, particularly an eagle flying. And as I allowed it all to flow the sadness disappeared." - Sylvia

After our *Inti Raymi* ceremony the masters commenced with the explanation of the fire element.

I N R I "Igne natura renovatur integra"

"Only through fire, nature is renewed"

When fire touches the world, as slayer or destroyer, it is not to punish but is a purifying, sanctifying fire that turns the impure or stagnant to ashes. Fire renews, it vivifies.

There is much wisdom in the ancient World. The Masons, Templar's, Rosicrucian's, all tell of a 'blazing sword'. In the Holy Bible, Divine displays are accompanied by fire. It was through the fire and the 'sword' that Moses purified his people and the surrounding polluting elements. Moses led his people with the assistance of a steam column in the day and a fire column in the night.

The Etruscans raised alters to worship fire, believed to embody the solar and immaterial energies. Vesta, the Roman fire goddess, reflection of the Greek Goddess Hestia, was worshipped as the home goddess.

In the Andean Tradition fire is the representation of *INTI* (the sun) and the Light of creation of human beings, and is sacred.

The fire in our lives pushes us to an authentic path, leading to full embodiment of potential and accomplishments. It helps overcome trials inspired by violent emotions. It sanctifies us and awakens our sleeping energy or *Illapa* (*Kundalini*) touching each one of our internal cores or *Nawis* (*Chakras*).

Rubies represent Solar Fire and Opals, Mystical Fire.

Fire is the most beneficial and wonderful source of heat and light. It encourages, the warmth of sacrifice as giving. It is Love in motion. Matter spreads when heated, and we expand and grow when touched by our Divine internal fire.

On the other hand, fire seems to be the most dangerous of all the elements but it is also the element which produces real transmutation. Fire is an active element but it is ordered. Its force appears to be dangerous; but only because we are not conscious of it.

In every religion, fire is the third party of the Trinity, representing transformation, as Holy Spirit, Shiva or Horus. Fire is alchemy. It transforms human beings to their essence state, wrenching away matter, returning them to the Prime Rhythm, Universal flow or Divine Movement. The quality associated with fire is daring. The trials of daring are powerful ones. If we are friends with fire we become recipients of its capacity to overcome these trials.

To temper iron we forge it with fire and then put it into water, oil and other substances. For us, we must take a walk through the trials of Fire and the trials of Water to begin living.

Since the early workshops I became aware of the distinction between our sentimental feelings and our emotions. In the English language we tend to use the word emotion to encompass all our feelings. Some people discern feeling as being a physical experience, associating it with sensation. But in Spanish, feelings (sentimental feeling associated with water) and emotions (strong emotions associated with fire) are distinctly different words and states.

If we become friends with fire and work with it, we overcome our fears and are able to cope with trial, both psychic and physical e.g. if a house is burning, we dare to overcome our fear of the flames in order to save the people inside. In daily living, if we need to act boldly, we succeed with the assistance of fire.

It is impossible to work with fire and experience no change. Primitive man, our ancestors, changed their existence completely when they discovered fire. As man learnt to dominate fire, his lifestyle, diet and environment changed. Today with the development of Atomic 'fire', our lives may again face massive change, one way or another.

After practising with fire for a time, everything seems brighter, stronger, and then we begin to access the power that our fire brings us.

Listening to *Kamaq Wageaq* and *Hatun Runa* share this information I realised fire and I were already friends. After the first workshop I attended, I returned to a life that had become stagnant, through no fault of anyone else, and that the fire had given me the courage to embrace change. Those changes had not been easy but I became alive, thrilled by the arrival of a new day and the possibilities that it brought. I would draw many times over the years to come on fire, daring to make my dreams a reality, usually with great success, but always with a sense of living authentically through this Divine Alchemist.

The emotional energies, relating to fire, are strong, powerful and can move human nature to destruction, if our internal fire is mismanaged. I refer to them as the shadow of fire; they include rage, jealousy, hatred, revenge and fear.

If our fire is stagnant or suppressed, we find ourselves locked into these destructive emotions, but working with fire will release us into courage, daring and fearlessness. Creating and experiencing the extraordinary is possible. We go beyond our perceived limitations, accessing our full capacity and potential.

Fire takes on many forms, from external fire which brings heat, through its energetic vibration, to the sacred fire of saints and masters. Through antiquity, all sacred spaces, temples, churches, mosques, burnt sacred fire in all spiritual and religious beliefs. In ancient times these fires were tended and kept alive by woman. Men wielded fire and women nurtured it, they were the keepers of sacred fire.

In the Andean Tradition fire is indeed sacred. Fire is the element which can transmute and change all other elements, used in our ceremonies with great reverence. When our offerings are burnt they are taken from the physical dimension to *Ille Tecsi Wiracocha*, directly to the Divine.

The highest expression of fire in the physical reality is service. When fire has journeyed through all the levels of human consciousness, it finally takes the expression of Divine service to humanity. Energetically it can be understood as the journey of the *Illapa* (called the *Kundalini* in other traditions) energy from the base of the spine through all the *Nawis* (*Chakras* in other traditions), out of the crown *Nawi*, through our body centres to connect to the Divine Self. Once this has transpired, the purpose of life for a human being has one main satisfying motivation, to bring Divine consciousness to other Humans.

After observing fire, I realised something obvious - fire is always vertical. Water finds its own balance horizontally and fire always reaches upwards. When I realised this I understood why fire is perceived to be holy. It, like us, reaches upwards towards the Creator.

Our material body contains the Earth and Water elements, although water to a greater degree as we are three quarters water, the same as our planet earth. The air as oxygen expands through us into our blood and nervous systems. We have a body temperature of thirty-six degrees, reflecting the fire in the physical as temperature and energy. All these elements interconnect and manifest life, but there are other non-physical elements that produce these structures. The first is the fifth element which we express as love. This element in turn generates the sixth element as intuition and imagination. We often disregard imagination but all imagery produced by imagination is a reality, a virtual reality certainly, but a reality never the less.

The experience of the fifth and sixth elements is a journey that manifests with time, beginning with the first four elements.

"This workshop offered many opportunities to reflect on areas of my life I had ignored for a long time. We worked with the elements daily and I became aware of their immense clearing and healing powers. I started seeing my surroundings and nature through new eyes and finding joy and pleasure there, while being excited about my newly found life and way forward. I became aware of the little things that I took for granted.

I recall leaving the venue early evening after the workshop ended, noticing every bush and flower on the road side, seeing their beauty and brightness and the variety of colours they displayed. Nature suddenly became alive revealing herself to me more clearly and brightly.

I was immersed in gratitude and joy for the first time in many years. The experience moved and transformed me, I felt blessed.

I connected to the elements daily, clearing myself of many things and shifting my consciousness to another level.

I was fortunate to live close to the ocean where I often went for solace, walking along the beach allowing Mother Ocean to clear me of my heaviness and pain. The wind would join by blowing a breeze at the appropriate time, clearing my energy field and the sun lovingly nurturing my body with warmth, while the steadfastness of Table Mountain was visible in the distance, unmoved by the harshness of life. The more I worked with the elements, the more I was embraced by them." - Linda

CHAPTER SIX

CEREMONY & AYNI

That same year I underwent the second level initiation. It was a very different experience to the first initiation a year earlier since this was a teaching process whereas the former had been an experiential process. The various initiation levels can be categorised as such.

DESPACHO

Although I cannot share the specifics of this initiation, it dealt with a ceremony called the *Despacho*.

Before we begin ceremony of any description in the Andean Tradition we always invoke the directions. The invocation of the directions is honouring and 'calling' the energies from the entire universe. In the Andean Tradition the perception of the Universe is a dynamic structuring of many dimensions of existence. So everything is covered in the invocation; what lies above us, below us, behind us, in front of us, to our left, to our right and within our interior.

Represented are the hanaq Pacha or dimensions of Spirit and the Creator (above), the *Uju pacha* or underworld (below), the four directions are their corresponding elements (North - air, South - water, East - fire and West - earth) and *Nojan kani kani*, the 'I am that I am' presence in our interior. The invocation of the directions creates space and the energetic environment in which ceremony takes place.

The directions are usually invoked in *Quechua,* the language of an indigenous people of the Andes. We begin by facing East (the direction from which the sun rises), we acknowledge this direction and then we turn to our right to begin the invocation with the south. Herewith, follows the translated version of the invocations in English:

Winds of the South
Come to us, receive us, bless us and give us the welcome of your power, strength and energy. Hatun Amaru, great serpent, Sacha Mama, great serpent – mother of the waters. Bless us. Provide us with good work, good wisdom and good love in all parts of the world.

We turn to our right to face the West.

Winds of the West
Come to us, receive us, bless us and give to us the welcome of your power, strength and

energy. Jaguars of light, come to us, receive us and heal us. Great rainbow help us in our journey through the three worlds – Uju Pacha, Kay Pacha and Hanaq Pacha. Teach us and guide us down the road of life. Provide us with good work and good love in all parts of the world.

We turn to our right to face the North

Winds of the North
Good winds of change, come to us, receive us, bless us and give us the welcome of your power, strength and energy. To all the masters – Kuraq Akulleq – give us power, strength and energy; make us owners of your great spirit. Prince of the rainbow - give us your wisdom. Divine hummingbird - come to us, receive us and give us good work, good wisdom in all parts of the world.

We again turn to the right to face the East again

Winds of the East
Come to us, receive us bless us and give us your energy. Keep us in our journey. Royal Condor – sacred eagle – give us the gift of your vision, give us your heart. Help us to bring healing to all nations. Provide us with good work, good knowledge, good wisdom and good love in all parts of the world.

We then kneel on the ground with our foreheads touching the Earth

Pachamama (Earth)

To the blessed Mother Earth, Pachamamita – receive us, hold us, bless us and give us your waters and food of every day. To all the Apus (mountains) come to us, receive us – Asangate Apu, Salkantay Apu, Chicon Apu, Kilomanjaro Apu (highest mountain on our continent), Magaliesberg Apu (mountain range closest to where the invocation is taking place) – give us your power.

We stand and reach up with our arms into the sky.

Ille Tecsi Wiracocha (Our Creator)

Ille Tecsi Wiracocha, Pacha Camac, Great Spirit – you who are known by many names but you are The One with no name. We thank you for the creation and our lives, which you have given to us. To all the stars – the Pleiades, the Southern Cross – come to us, enlighten us and join us in our ceremony because we are celebrating what we will become.

For the final direction we cross our arms over our heart centre (chests)

The Great Nojan Kani Kani

There are no words spoken as this direction is honoured in silence. It is the internal presence of being within each of us.

Once the invocations are complete we begin with the ceremony in question.

During the initiation I learnt the theoretical and practical process of the *Despacho* ceremony, but it was only through its use, over time, that I came to fully understand and appreciate this sacred and ancient ritual.

The *Despacho* is an offering of gratitude for what life gives us or gratitude in anticipation for a petition whose manifestation we await. It is performed by an Andean priest or *Altomisayoq* (third level initiate) through an element to the creator (*Ille Tecsi Wiracocha* – the one without name). Either an earth, air, fire or water *Despacho* can be performed, varying slightly to better reflect qualities of the element but the basic process remains the same. There are over 400 different variations of the *Despacho* – for different occasions, or depending on the area of the Andes where the practice is taking place. In the different villages of the Andes readily available ingredients to their area are used, and the content can alter considerably. The basic structure however remains the same from one area to another and the power of intention is the force which brings the *Despacho* to realization.

At this point I had never examined nor experienced ritual seriously, so I had few opinions but again with experience I came to understand more.

Ceremony and ritual are the process of bringing order to create specific energetic conditions and environments. I sometimes feel in this process I am reflecting, most humbly, the Divine process of Creation, bringing order into chaos. In doing so there is an honoring and remembering. In the Andean tradition ceremony is used both to give gratitude to the Divine and for manifestation of requests, for the community. It is, at a human level, an act of service to our brothers and sisters.

The elements are given certain symbolic credence in these rituals, pertaining to the specific nature of the request. For example, the earth would be used in a ceremony of gratitude to give thanks for physical, material or bodily manifestations. Water would be used for the softer more intuitive, emotional or sentimental feminine issues. Air would be used for gratitude of mental, intellectual and communicative issues, and the fire for issues relating to courage and power,

The *Despacho* is a public ceremony, creating a Mandala of natural elements placed onto a large white sheet of paper, folded into nine sections. These sections symbolize vertically the three worlds: *Uju Pacha* (under world, internal world or sub conscious), *Kay Pacha* (the physical reality in which we live, the sensory world or human consciousness) and *Hanaq Pacha* (the spirit realms, supreme world or super consciousness). These three worlds are further represented horizontally in the past, present and future. It symbolizes the dynamic interaction between the three worlds and the 'time zones'. This demonstrates perfectly the Andean Traditions understanding of the universe, an understanding that does not contain space and time, but rather one continual manifestation of existence, a dynamic interaction of time and space in perpetuity.

The centre of the *Despacho,* where the offering is created, represents the void from which creation emanates into the three worlds. We call it the *Tecsi Muyo*, the centre of order or chaos, depending on how it is viewed; it is the most dynamic area, where destruction or creation of all that exists takes place.

The *Despacho* covers all aspects, places, and directions; nothing in the Universe is unaccounted for. The most distant stars, the Milky Way and all the planets are represented. Not only the heavenly bodies are accounted for but also the intelligence , which emanates from those distant places also.

During the *Despacho,* those attending can place wishes or desires into a Coca leaf, which is then placed into the *Despacho* by the priest. The wish is reinforced by the intention of the priest and sent to the superior energy of *Ille Tecsi Wiracocha* (God). From my personal experience the turn-around time for the manifestation, born from my wishes placed into the Coca leaf, is fast.

"For several days I had been unable to capture the lioness we were filming doing anything of interest. Our frustration levels were rising. I had to do something. It occurred to me that I should perform a Despacho to the Pachamama and ask for her intervention. We returned to camp and that night I did the Despacho. The next morning as we were driving out of camp there she was. The lioness was hunting and the light was beautiful. We captured some really amazing footage." - Herbert

At the end of the *Despacho* the priest cleanses the attendants' energy with both the *Despacho* and his or her *Mesa*. This removes the heavy energy from the persons' psyche. This energy is then burnt or buried with the *Despacho*. The first Despacho on a property is buried, subsequent ones are burnt. The Earth or Fire element is able to transmute this heavy energy of the Despacho into positive energy and return it to us in renewed form.

A *Pampamisayoq*, second level initiate, is prepared to perform Despacho and it is considered an important act on the path of service to the community. There are other rituals performed in different areas of the Andes called; *Pagos, Pagapuy, Tinkuy, Challa* or *Mesada* and although they are always performed in the service of humanity, they are hosted on a private, individual basis. They are not performed in public for the whole community, as is the *Despacho*.

Generally the timing for ceremony is related to the phases of the moon and the seasonal cycles. The equinoxes, solstices and full moon are considered important energetic times, and the influences of the moon are taken into consideration always. When the moon is growing (waxing) the energies around our planet are gaining momentum and are at their strongest – this is perceived to be a good time for the planting of crops, beginning of new projects etc. This period will bring quick growth. When the moon is diminishing (waning), the energies are depleting, and lessening in strength. This becomes the ideal time to bring things to closure or to ensure a slow growth. For example, hair that is cut when the moon is waning will grow slowly. When the moon is full, she is at her most powerful and this is the time for clearest connection and the quickest manifestations.

Solstices and equinoxes are important reminders of the seasonal changes, each offering the perfect time for certain actions, attitudes and intentions.

There are specific elements that relate to the Solstices and Equinoxes. The dates given below are for equinox and solstice in the Southern Hemisphere:

Date	Event	Element
21 March	Autumn Equinox	Water
21 June	Winter Solstice	Air
21 September	Spring Equinox	Earth
21 December	Summer Solstice	Fire

The specific element relating to the date would determine the type of Despacho that would be performed.

Ceremony performed to the elements in the Andean Tradition, has played a big role because of the geographical location of the indigenous people. High up in the Andes survival is not easy and without the full co-operation of the elements, the very livelihood of the community is placed in dire risk. In order to better understand this statement it is necessary to look at the 'law of *Ayni*' practised throughout the Andes.

AYNI

Ayni is a Quechua word and refers to the sacred law of reciprocity; it is one of the foundation principles of the Andean Tradition. This principle has been very important in ensuring social balance within the Andean societies, dating back thousands of years. It is simple but with profound and far reaching expressions. It is the process of giving, supported by the universal law of cause and effect.

Within Ayni, once one's own simple needs have been fulfilled, all excess is shared. It is the process of giving, without being asked and the fulfillment for the giver comes through the satisfaction of giving. There is no expected or hidden motivation within the act of giving. The Universal law of cause and effect ensures that when the giver has need, that need is fulfilled through the same law.

Simply put, A gives to B, and when A has need, A too will receive, according to the sacred laws of reciprocity but not necessarily from B, most likely though C, D or E. In the West we tend to lean more towards direct energy exchange. A gives to B and B must reciprocate. It seems the perception here is that no debt or obligation is incurred. However, it often becomes a process of tallying the quantity of giving and is often a self-imposed prison of service to self-first. We become so concerned in making certain that we receive equally, or more than, what we have given, that the joy of giving is lost to us.

With the principle of *Ayni*, giving is imparted with an open heart, an expression of joy simply for the sake of itself. It is the understanding of Universal Law and the trust of it that ensures the success and perpetuation of *Ayni*. To ensure the energy of Ayni continues, after receiving it we must also give. We cannot hold onto it or the cycle is broken.

Ayni is practiced not only among people but within nature, and the Universe. Andean Tradition ceremonial practice is guided by this principle. What has, by the Western mind been mistaken as pagan or idol worship is in fact *Ayni* in action. Earth provides us with abundance and supports our lives so, when we have excess, we give back to the Earth. Hence in our ceremonies we give to our *Pachamama,* wine and sweets. They are physical objects but symbolize the reciprocation of what we have received.

Nature is living; all the elements are conscious dynamic forces, each governing and influencing specific qualities and areas of us and life. When we interact consciously, through *Ayni*, with nature – she responds. The result is a harmonious interchange with nature and the universe. Life flows!

Within the Andean tradition, work is considered sacred and honorable. The nature of the work, so long as it is honest, serves the community and in the long run, humanity, is irrelevant. According to the sacred principle of *Ayni*, to be lazy is a form of theft. There is a basic underlying belief that through productivity and active participation we will provide for ourselves or be provided for.

In the west we horde, the more we horde the greater our show of power, but this is not true power as its based in material possession and not on our relationship with ourselves, where we can take our security from within and from our connection *to Ille Tecsi Wiracocha*.

In the Andes, excess is shared, often through festivity. When there is too much for immediate use it is time to entertain the community. *Ayni* promotes individual freedom, through independence, with a reciprocal responsibility to each community member. *Ayni* requires we are able to receive as well as give and is dependent on our community interaction. Total independence from the community becomes impractical and dangerous if the individual separates themselves from their community. Separateness can create resentment, isolation and misunderstandings. The psychological effects can be devastating. The experience of shouldering burdens alone without the support of community, form an isolated, lonely existence where fears of not having enough can govern our very perceptions and existence. Many of our modern societies promote isolated existences, unsupported by community.

For successful practice of *Ayni*, there must be an understanding of oneness, the interconnection of all life forms as a part of one other. What we do to others and to nature, we do to ourselves. *Ayni* is the conscious dialogue, the inter-active reciprocation with all that exists.

If we build a stone wall, we honor the Earth for these materials, which are extension of her. Before we eat, we honor the Earth, the Air, the Water and the Fire who all played a role in providing our food. *Ayni* makes possible harmonious living with nature, where there is a gratitude and humility. Its expressions are a reflection of the highest forms of human nature in action.

With *Ayni* the energy of the giver is in what is given. If that energy is not reproduced, through the act of giving to another what you have received, the cycle of abundance is broken and that energy withers.

Ayni keeps us connected to nature as a part of her and ensures the constant flow of abundance in our lives. Fear of not having enough is no longer necessary.

Understanding the *Ayni* principal ceremony takes on new meaning. The Andean Tradition teaches that nature is the manifestation of creation in the physical dimension; it is a reflection of *Ille Tecsi Wiracocha's* creation and contains the universal flow which governs all of life. When we pay respects and offer love to nature, we honour *Ille Tecsi Wiracocha* and ourselves as a part of creation, as matter, which is governed and held within that universal flow.

Ceremony is prayer, connection, love and gratitude in action.

CHAPTER SEVEN

THE COSMOGONY, THE CREATOR, DUALITY & ASTROLOGY

In the Andean Tradition it is believed that before time the potential of everything was contained in the *'Tiqsimuyo'*, the Supreme Circle, the Void. The Supreme Lord *Nojan Kani Kani*, the one who was, is and will be, through *Ille Tecsi Wiracocha*, created order from chaos bringing about the Multi-Verses, Universes and the worlds of being.

Thus our world was created, inhabited by human beings and the animal and plant kingdoms. It is believed that the human was birthed into creation without consciousness and that the evolution of man is to grow in awareness and consciousness, continually expanding and deepening in order to return to and become one with The Creator. It is believed that this consciousness is attained through the star of enlightenment and love, Venus, known as *Lloque Chaska*.

The word of *Ille Tecsi Wiracocha*, is light contained in Spirit and the words of men are carried from our world to the realm of Spirit, and the word of *Ille Tecsi Wiracocha* is carried to us here on the Earth plane by a special messenger, the Condor, which is able to reach the great heights of the *Hanaq Pacha*.

And so from the teachings of the 'ancient ones,' who once walked our beloved planet comes the parable of the Hummingbird and the Condor.

Through the shifting sands of time the condor, like its brother the eagle, has fulfilled the role of Divine messenger, flying high into the heavens delivering the prayers, pleas and messages of humanity to the ear of the *Great Ille Tecsi Wiracocha*. Out of respect for the Divine Presence, the Condor would always avert his head, never looking into the eyes of the Creator.

One day the hummingbird, the smallest of all birds, asked the condor to allow him to journey to *Ille Tecsi Wiracocha*. The Condor smiled, replying that this was impossible as only he, the great Condor could fly to the heights necessary to connect with the Divine Presence.

Unbeknown to the Condor sometime later, as he prepared to fly into the heavens, the Hummingbird slipped undetected into his feathers. Keeping very still, the Hummingbird rode on the back of the Condor until the Condor began to approach the Divine. At the exact moment that the Condor averted his face, the Hummingbird peeped out and stared squarely into the face of the Creator. The Condor realised what had happened but could do nothing, it was too late.

So he had to acknowledge that there was one bird greater than himself, the hummingbird, who had looked into the eyes of *Ille Tecsi Wiracocha*. It also became known that the hummingbird in that moment was bathed in iridescent light, and henceforth its plumage shimmers with magnificent colour.

The Hummingbird had drunk the nectar from every flower and was therefore ready for enlightenment. The *Aumatas* (Andean masters) consider each flower with its distinct shape and colour, to be a representation of the unique beauty of different spiritual, mystic, initiating, esoteric or philosophic schools or lineages.

The nectar is the essence of each of these spiritual expressions and the hummingbird, with the profound knowledge of all these paths, is fully prepared to stand *before Ille Tecsi Wiracocha*. Likewise the human being searches endlessly for meaning, depth and understanding until he begins to comprehend the path to The Divine and the conciliation with himself.

THE THREE WORLDS

In order to better understand the Cosmogony of the Andean Tradition, we must understand the three worlds. Each of these worlds corresponds with different levels of our consciousness. They are the *Hanaq Pacha* relating to superior, higher conscious; the *Kay Pacha* to the mundane sensory consciousness of our physical, material reality; and the *Uju Pacha* to our internal sub-consciousness.

These worlds are living energetic realms. The *Kay Pacha* (our daily material reality) contains energy in form as matter, and so we perceive it as more 'real'. The energies of the Kay Pacha vibrate at a slower frequency than those of the Hanaq Pacha and so we perceive our physical reality as being solid. Although this realm is presented as physical matter it is in essence energy manifested, energy which is perceived by our higher senses.

The Hanaq Pacha (the realm of the super conscious, spirit) and the Uju Pacha (subconscious or underworld) are not presented as matter but retain their original energetic form making them no less real, they are simply unmasked and pure energy. These three realms do not relate to earth, heaven and hell as perceived in Christianity since the Andean perception is different.

The Hanaq Pacha

Thease are the realms of the Paradise Father, spirit beings and angels. It is a non - physical reality and can be accessed directly or via our super conscious. The animal totem or symbol of this realm is the Condor; a big, powerful bird. It is the messenger between the *Hanaq Pacha* and the *Kay Pacha*, between *Ille Tecsi Wiracocha* (God) and human beings. The Condor is also the symbol of peace.

The Andean Priest acts as a Condor, communing with the Upper Worlds and the beings that dwell there, through their expanded consciousness. This ability is used in the service of the community bringing guidance and healing through the connection with this heightened vibration frequency. The Andean Priest also takes the wishes and pleas of the community to the *Hanaq Pacha* requesting Divine Intervention. The experience of the priest in the *Despacho* ceremony is an excellent example of this.

When I, as the priest performing *Despacho*, commence the ceremony I always feel my consciousness being drawn inwards and upwards. A feeling of immense devotion and the honor of being in service to the community around me becomes very strong. There is sacredness and humility in the process. I have a strong presence of love both within and surrounding me. During the ceremony, each person is given a cocoa leaf into which they place their wishes or desires which is then presented to the priest. When I receive the cocoa leaf from the individual they are the only person that exists for me, they have my full focus and intention. There is no arrogance in this power, I am in service to the individual in front of me and wish it with my entire being. I hold the leaf to my third-eye, and in that moment what that person has put into the leaf is clear, like words written on a page. With the purest intention of love, I blow it straight into the *Hanaq Pacha* to be received by *Ille Tecsi Wiracocha*. The leaf is then placed into the *Despacho,* and as this happens I hear the words of *Ille Tecsi Wiracocha* responding to the individuals' request. The power of this experience for the priest is immense and received with humility.

After the second level initiation, my psychic and intuitive abilities grew enormously. This is natural for all initiates. Although some people are stronger in certain areas, the conscious expansion of our communication with spirit is a natural growth and form of communication. I live now in a reality where I walk between the three worlds, in communion with all of them. I am not locked into a third dimensional experience of reality and these interactions are so simple and natural, like conversing with another person.

The Kay Pacha

The *Kay Pacha* is the realm in which we live physically. Its totem is the Puma, the feline. From the beginning, I had a strong connection with the Earth. My awareness of the other elements grew over time. This connection begins with the realization of self as a part of nature. In most western societies we live separate to and beyond nature. Our environments are designed to separate us from the elements. Our homes, our offices, our shopping malls, our transport are all weather proof and our contact with the elements is entirely controlled. We no longer live in nature. We need to make an effort to be outdoors, to be in nature.

This disconnection is symbolic and real. We become desensitized when disconnected from nature. Also if the external realitys' are reflective of our internal natures there is disconnection from ourselves. The Andean tradition offers a practical way to re-establish that connection and to maintain it, in spite of the fact that our physical world is made up of brick, mortar, technology and petrol fumes.

That conscious connection, together with a deepened understanding of myself makes it possible for me to live a gentler more harmonious and fearless existence.

Using the elements I am able to balance the relationship between mind, body, emotions and energy. I reach beyond myself to feel a sense of security and of safety in the world, not based on the material but rather on a sense of belonging and simplicity in my state of being.

This connection to nature is not purely etheric. It has very real manifestations at times. In my home, in the centre of a built up city I have, on occasion encountered small animals including a bat and a chameleon at times when their presence is totally nonsensical but symbolically appropriate to my circumstances. Other than these occasions, it has been many years since I have laid eyes on these creatures, and certainly not in a town house environment.

Several years ago, we hosted an Andean workshop in the Cape. At the time we were blessed with a heat wave with temperatures in excess of forty-two degrees Celsius. It was hot and I was experiencing an enormous rise in Illapa (*Kundalini*) energies.

On two separate days, just before the rise in my Illapa energy, on stone stairs outdoors I encountered a Cape Cobra sunning itself. This snake is deadly and on both occasions I was close enough to look into its eyes. A step further and I would have walked on it.

On the first day, after gazing at me for a moment it simply turned and slid away. On the second day, the exact same thing happened. Clearly I did not get the message the first time. And then the rise in *Illapa* began.

Illapa or *Kundalini* refers to an inherent energy, situated at the base of our spines. This energy, at certain points in consciousness in the individual, rises up the spine as two separate streams, one masculine, and one feminine. They entwine themselves around the *Chakras* - vortexes of energy, pushing skyward. They are depicted as two entwined serpents, rising up in figures of eight, over a central column. This symbol has been adopted by modern medicine but is the ancient depiction of the *Illapa, Kundalini* movement.

When we are in harmony with nature and the elements, we are not only supported energetically but nature responds differently to us. It does not perceive us as an alien, an outsider but rather as a part of itself. As such the plants and animals respond differently to us. They do not shy away or hide as they do normally. We are accepted as a part of what we actually are, another expression of nature.

The Uju Pacha

The final realm in the Andean Tradition is the *Uju Pacha*. This, for me, has been the most mysterious relationship and the one that has taken the longest to form.

The *Uju Pacha* is the subconscious state of being and the totem guardian of this realm is the snake. For a long time I did not understand this realm, a reflection of my unexplored subconscious self. It is perceived existing inside of the Earth, referred to as the Underworld and within ourselves, our sub conscious. This is not a 'hell' realm or a 'bad' place. It is simply another consciousness environment. It is governed by a consciousness or being, and the energy is feminine.

"My first encounter with 'her' came at a most unexpected time. After my initial visit to Peru, I had fallen in love with the place and the work of the artisans. With two good friends, we undertook to import some of these items to South Africa. One partner in this venture and I flew over on our first buying trip. This is not a first world environment where we could view a catalogue over the Internet, so we traveled to the markets, choosing items and bargaining for them. The noises, smells and colors were fantastic and I was immersed in a world of sensory stimulation. We loved it but it was tiring. Our shopping took us from Peru to Bolivia, where the bright woven fabrics are manufactured. We shopped till we almost dropped. We then needed to get all our purchases on a flight to South Africa before we headed back to Peru. Our flight back to Peru was booked for a Saturday. We were both looking forward to this, as we had flu, finding the climate in Bolivia cold and difficult, and our visas were about to expire.

We had an export agent assist us with the paper work but try as we might we could not get police or customs clearance for our goods. We were told they would be granted the morning we were due to leave Bolivia. This meant we had to transport 1000's of meters of fabrics, and many kilos of other goods to the airport, only to find on arrival that the information was incorrect and no such clearance was forthcoming. We were stuck. We ended up leaving all this merchandise in the airport lockup area, with no real security and in the hands of our translator, who we had known for less than three days. This was with a promise of her help when clearance was granted, if it was granted.

We left Bolivia. On arrival in Cuzco, Peru I immediately contacted Kamaq Wageag and asked for his assistance. It was simply blocked and no matter what we did nothing had budged. We were really in a bind.

Kamaq Wageag's response puzzled me. He said that we had never received permission from the Uju Pacha to enter Bolivia nor to remove these items from Bolivia. He told us to make amends immediately. He told us to make an offering to the Uju Pacha and for this we needed a river. The only river we knew was the Urubamba River in Pisac, an hour drive by taxi. We gathered what we needed, jumped into a taxi and underwent a hair rising trip to Pisac. Never tell a Cuzco taxi driver you are in a hurry, he will take you seriously.

We arrived, and began our ceremony. I was surprised to encounter intuitively the lady of the Uju Pacha. She addressed me saying that I must be aware of my mistake and not repeat it. I must acknowledge her and honour her in future. I agreed willingly. We did not discuss merchandise and when she had finished reprimanding me, she dismissed me. I wasn't sure what to think but jumped back in the taxi and took a slower drive back to Cuzco.

On arrival, there was a message from the translator in Bolivia. Against all odds, police and customs clearance had been granted and our merchandise was on its way to South Africa awaiting collection on our return home.

I hadn't realized the encounter would be so tangible, both in the effect and in the communication itself. I would come to recognize the problems and difficulties that arise from the Uju Pacha, for me and others." - Sally

"Herbert is a fellow initiate in the Andean Tradition and a wild life cameraman. He had been, working for months in the African Bush, living out of a tent. Through his expansion in consciousness he has become a competent animal communicator, using these skills to track the right animal at the right time, and capturing it all on film. He went through a period of frustration where he felt his intuitive skills had abandoned him and nobody wanted to talk to him, especially the lions. We had a phone conversation around this time and I had the sense of the blockage the Uju Pacha can wreak if dishonored. My friend assured me that he had honored the Earth and the Apus but had not made an offering to the Uju Pacha. I suggested he did.

Within a few days he sent a message to say that all was well and the flow had returned to himself and his work."

It is not that the Uju Pacha is a negative force; it is a powerful realm of the planetary sub consciousness which influences our daily reality on many levels, requiring acknowledgment and conscious interaction to gain its co-operation and support. I have come to hold a great affection for the Uju Pacha and the feminine power that governs there. She has helped me many times over the years.

THE CREATOR

In the Andean Tradition the Supreme Force is *Nojan Kani Kani*. This is The Internal Presence of Being, which exists in us all and in all that exists. It signifies 'I am that I am' and is a statement of presence. At this level of existence there is no separation; all is inter-connected with everything else.

Ille Tecsi Wiracocha is perceived as the loving Creator of our universe. This means the 'the One with no name' and it is *Ille Tecsi Wiracocha* who manifested and maintains creation. This is the expression of Divinity. *Ille Tecsi Wiracocha* contains within both the feminine and masculine and all the aspects of those two energies. It is not referred to by gender.

The masculine expression of Divine Creative Force for planet earth and our solar system is *Inti*, the Sun, also known as the *Solar Logos*. This is the perceived expression of the Divine Masculine within our Solar System. When the Incas paid respect to the Sun, they did not worship it as a ball of fire but rather as the Being who makes life and its manifestations possible. *Inti* is a living energy with its own consciousness.

The Divine Feminine energy is expressed through *Pachamama* - Earth, Nature and through *Mama Quilla* the Moon. The Earth is the nurturing aspect of the feminine and the moon is the inspiring aspect of it. Again these are living beings, energies manifested in form containing infinite consciousness and wisdom. At this level of manifestation the Sun, the Moon and the Earth, perceived separation has taken place and duality exists. It is a perceived separation because at the highest energetic levels all is interconnected. This duality is interdependent. For balance we require the Sun, the Earth and the Moon. Light cannot be seen without shadow to give a background to its illumination.

The *Inti Raymi* ceremony, which was mentioned earlier under the teachings of the Fire element, is conducted in the Southern Hemisphere at the Winter Solstice in the month of June and in the Northern Hemisphere the Winter Solstice is in December.

The Sun, as this expression of Divinity, is at its most distant point from the planet at the Winter Solstice. The ceremony is held at Sun rise and is both a celebration and a welcoming of the Sun's movement closer to the Southern Hemisphere of the planet. In this ceremony offerings of fruit and products of the Earth, '*Chicha*', or corn beer, and wine, are made to the Sun. The Sun's first rays are 'captured' into the energetic heart centre of those present, strengthening the Divine Spark within us. This ceremony also demonstrates the simple beauty of the *Ayni* principle in action.

The moon, *Mama Quilla* is honored each time she reaches fullness through *Despacho* Ceremony. As mentioned previously the evolution of humans happens through water and fire, governed by the moon and the sun respectively.

The Earth forms one of the foundation elements of our being and is honored in *every* ceremony performed. Without Earth there would be no platform for physical existence.

The general religious perception is that God is outside of us, however in the Andean Tradition we recognize ourselves as a part of creation and creation as an extension of Divinity. We go within to find God. *Ille Tecsi Wiracocha* is accessed in the space of Divine harmony and order within.

According to the Andean Tradition the purpose of our existence is our journey to the Creator. In other traditions this is called the journey to enlightenment or the path to illumination. This is a dual process, the focused journey into ourselves and the external expansion upwards of our consciousness. But if God is within, why are we expanding upwards, growing towards the light as the trees and plants do? The answer is simple - with expanded consciousness we are able to go deeper and higher. In the Andean Tradition it is perceived that *Ille Tecsi Wiracocha, Source* is in a specific location in the Universe.

We as Andean priests are priests of nature. The elements offer us simple and effective solutions to the problems of disharmony, chaos and imbalance. Humanity does not have a set path; it is path that we create as we walk. There are the universal laws by which man and nature are governed, including the law of cause and effect. This law is also reflected in physics through the understanding that for every action there is an equal and opposite reaction. So we must take responsibility for what we create. When we take responsibility and are in acceptance of ourselves, and our lives we access the flow and the power to change ourselves, and our reality. If the Divine Creator is our point of existence, then even if there is no set path, there is a destination.

Through this journey only love and *Ille Tecsi Wiracocha* manifest in the human heart. This truth makes us, as human beings, alive now, the promoters of this life and the protectors of our own evolution.

DUALITY

During one of these beautiful *Inti Raymi* ceremonies I received simple but valuable understanding of the nature of duality on this planet. This intuitive teaching was given to me by *Inti – Father Sun*.

I was shown that because in our solar system we have only one sun, half of our planet at any given time is in darkness and half in light. This is not symbolic of the duality that exists but the reason for it. I was shown that in other solar systems where two or more suns are contained, duality does not exist, and the process and purpose of life experience is very different.

This duality exists at all levels of creation in our Solar System.

ASTRONOMY AND ASTROLOGY

The makeup of the Universe, and more locally our Solar system play a big role in the Andean Tradition with astronomy and astrology influencing many areas of life. From the architectural layout of cities created during the reign of the Inka Empire, to the appropriate day of having your hair cut or '*rutuchi*' (Quechua word for cutting hair). The many fascinating ruins in the region of the Incan Empire in South America reflect this.

This is not a superstitious relationship with the planets, but rather one in which optimal life flow, where energy and circumstances are accessed. For example the days of the week are pertinent as they each reflect a planet; those planets in turn have specific influence in their qualities. The naming the week days after the sun, the moon and the five visible planets (Mars, Mercury, Jupiter, Venus and Saturn) was an acknowledgment of the Roman gods of the same names. Today the Latin influences in the English language and other languages still reflect the names of the planets:

Monday is named after the moon, which is feminine. It is a good day to deal with sentimental, emotional and psychic issues, family - especially children and occult work relating to women. (In Spanish *'Lunes'* is Monday and Luna is the moon)

Tuesday is named after Mars, the Roman god of war and is a good day to work with issues needing strength and determined, action especially economic issues, and those where dismissal is necessary (In Spanish *'Martes'* is Tuesday and *Marte* is Mars).

Wednesday is named after Mercury, the Roman messenger god and is good for intellectual and mental issues, all communication and expansive actions. (In Spanish Wednesday is *'Miécoles'* and Mercury is *Mercurio*)

Thursday is named after Jupiter, the supreme Roman god and is a good day for exploration, expansion, adventure, investigation and seeking more profound understanding. (In Spanish Thursday is *'Jueves'* and Jupiter is *Júpiter*)

Friday is named after Venus, the Roman goddess of love and is strictly for matters relating to sentimental emotion, harmony and unconditional love. It is a day of direct but gentle interaction. (In Spanish *'Viernes'* is Friday and Venus is *Venus*)

Saturday is named after Saturn and Saturnus is the Roman god of agriculture. It is a good day for self-examination, life direction, all psychic matters and consciousness. (In Spanish Saturday is *Sábado* and Saturn is *Saturno*)

Sunday is named after the Sun, which is Masculine. It is a good day for political and economic issues, areas relating to intimacy, work, prosperity and study. (In Spanish *Sol* is the sun, and Sunday is *Domingo*. After the Spanish invasion of Peru the day of the sun was changed to honour the Spanish leaders, who were always greeted with the title 'Dom' and in Quechua, the language of the Incas Sunday is **'Intichaw'** and the sun itself is *'Inti'*".)

In the Rosicrucian philosophy, the planets are associated with the main organs of the human body: lungs with Mercury, kidneys with Venus, liver with Jupiter, gall bladder with Mars, Spleen with Saturn, and the Sun is associated with the heart. In the Andean tradition the Sun, as mentioned previously, is considered a manifestation of Divine consciousness in our solar system, and the heart centre is considered the centre of our being. Through the heart centre we are able to access our Divine selves and the fifth element, which is perceived as unconditional love, the expression of *Ille Tecsi Wiracocha* (God).

In the Andean Tradition the Southern Cross and the Pleiades are acknowledged repeatedly in ceremonies and in the teachings. They are perceived as our cosmic origin as human beings. We came from the Pleiades originally and traveled via Mars and then Venus through the Southern Cross to reach the Earth. It's believed the Pleiadians are the protectors of Earth and humanity from negative extra-terrestrial forces, whose interest in Earth and her inhabitants are not in our best interests. In the sacred Andean Tradition astrology recognizes thirteen star signs, in both the solar and lunar systems, which was the system of the *Inka* cosmology.

Human beings as a group, emanate a powerful frequency of cosmic energy, which is constantly observed from outer space by our extra-terrestrial brothers. They wonder at the expansion and power of it. This vital cosmic energy, is perceived because it can be measured and has an atmosphere. This energy is used to access the time and space of the universe to alter reality. In the wrong hands it would create chaos in the universe.

This is the reason Earth and her inhabitants are so important cosmically and also why we have attracted great guides, avatars and spiritual masters over the ages, all bringing a message of wisdom to help us emanate positive cosmic frequencies as a group. It is in our best interests and those of our universe and our Creator that we do this successfully.

CHAPTER EIGHT

INTUITION & COMMUNITY

PAMPA MISAYOQ

My second initiation, the *Pampa Misayoq* priesthood initiation, brought with it, again, much change and new responsibilities. This time on the physical level my life grew but the structure created in the preceding year, remained much the same. My internal self, however was transformed and this reflected into my abilities as a healer and a psychic.

I began channelling, receiving messages from spirit and various guides for myself, clients and friends. Initially this happened as I performed healings but soon the information flowed even when I was moving through my day. The messages would come through clairaudience (internal hearing 'inside' my head). Initially this was my strongest link to spirit but over several years my other psychic senses developed, encompassing visual and sensory perceptions.

One of the first times this happened with a client I felt great resistance. The client was an elderly lady, a retired Naturopath who suffered from Tinnitus (ringing in the ears). As I performed healing on her, Spirit told me that to reduce the effects of the Tinnitus she should stop listening to the Wireless so much. 'Wireless' is not a word I use in my vocabulary, I would say radio. At the end of the session I asked tentatively whether she listened to the Radio much. She replied that it was her constant companion with one in the car, kitchen, bathroom, lounge and bedroom.

Feeling a little more confident I passed this message on to her and was greeted with the response "Don't be ridiculous". I was devastated, hurt and felt stupid. Several years later I read an article, printed in a national natural health magazine, regarding the effects of various 'waves' on our well-being. They discussed the negative frequency of television, microwaves, cell phones and radios. At the time it was ground breaking information, but now we are able to buy gadgets to counter-act these effects and it is commonly accepted as fact.

It was a good lesson in trusting myself and this inexplicable form of guidance I was receiving. It is important to note though that the confirmation in this instance came years after the event, trust and faith had to come first.

During the *Pampa Misayoq* initiation an exercise was performed to test our intuitive powers. I had failed the test. I learnt of this later, when in Peru for the first time, the exercise was repeated and the result was very different. *Kamaq Wageaq* gently and humbly presented to me, in private, the two different results. It was a confirmation of my growth over the months following the second initiation.

ESTABLISHING A COMMUNITY

My changed responsibilities at that time related back to the first encounter I had with these Masters, when *Kamaq Wageag* asked me if I would assist by organizing workshops in South Africa. As mentioned before, I blithely agreed without considering what it entailed. Understanding began to dawn.

In the months when the masters were not in South Africa, their students continued to grow and change. We performed ceremonies at the various important planetary times; worked with the elements; and very importantly gave service to one another as a community, and to the greater community, as humanity. A community was birthed.

It sounds so simple and easy as I write it now but the process was very different. This group of people with whom I had begun this journey, had difficulty accepting me as a leader. I understood why. I was younger, female and less experienced in energy matters than some. I had no experience in leading a group into a map-less future but the die was cast and forward we moved. Some of those people remain and some have fallen away, choosing other directions. This experience taught me so much about human nature, idealism, peoples' perceptions of power and responsibility, their capacity for spiritual ambition and myself.

Twelve years later, through many 'teething pains', the community begins to resemble my initial vision. There is a sense of family and unity among the members, and most importantly there seems to be an understanding in the difference between their own 'shifts' and the community. The members are now more inclined to take responsibility for their perceptions and journey and not project onto the greater group. The consciousness that our perceptions of the external world are simply a reflection of our internal one has taken hold. This makes for greater supportive interaction and definite purpose.

"Like many others on the journey of expansion I read all the books and attended all the public talks, listened to enlightening CD's for years, which kept me inspired. But when I was introduced to the Andean Tradition in March of 2008, I was filled with a sense this is what I had been looking for all along. There were two things that made the difference.

Firstly, the people in the Andean tradition (who have integrated it as their way of life) carry a lightness and compassion which envelopes you with love. They are still dealing with normal life dramas and experience, the same setbacks as the rest of us, but the difference is in their response. There is a steady fearlessness and events are not personal. On occasion when someone reacts unconsciously rather than respond, they seem to bounce back almost immediately.

I sense the Andean Tradition teaches us about power, and the perspective to use it productively.

The second difference is that the insights of the Andean Tradition are available to anyone. There is no hierarchy in knowing – there is no 'secret'. One progresses through the initiations in stages to allow time to integrate and practice the insights and principles. The more experienced people have no ego about where they are and what they know, and there is authentic enthusiasm to pass on their understanding. They don't rescue, try to save or remove your experiences; they share a perspective that they have used meaningfully in their own lives; you are encouraged to climb higher up the mountain to enjoy the beautiful view, and occasionally you rest and reflect on the last part of the journey. The more you climb, the smaller the 'dramas' you left behind appear. And all the while these lovely people climb ahead of you, encouraging you. Before you know it you have covered a lot of ground and it flowed continuously. The drama still emerges like rocks in the road but you just easily step over them. The best part is you keep your off centre sense of humour and the naughty glint in your eye. You don't hand these in at the door as you arrive." - *Donna*

"Although we gather acquaintances and friends through association with like-minded people in the Andean community, it is important to recognize that the primary purpose of the workshop, initiations, and the community is our own individual spiritual development and growth.

We are human and all make mistakes, have made them in the past, but it is possible to leave them behind and learn from them. We are all individuals and so our processes are all different. To have tolerance for one another and our differences makes for better interactions." - *Nela*

OLLANTAITAMBO

About 16 months after the second initiation, I traveled to Peru with a group of fellow South African's to undertake the third level initiation. The preparation for the trip and the journey itself brought extraordinary challenges. I organized and coordinated all the details for our group with contacts in Peru. The difficulties did not arise from the practical organization but from the human beings with whom I traveled. From this trip I understood that the Universe begins the preparation for initiation long before the day itself arrives. I had to learn to let go and accept what unfolded, instead of trying to fix things all the time.

I remember clearly stepping onto the soil of South America for the first time, the smells and the feeling. The moment my foot touched the ground in Buenos Aires I became very aware of the masters and felt their welcome and protection. They were both in Peru but certainly their frequency traveled. One of the first things *Kamaq Wageaq* said to me as we arrived in Peru was that he had felt our arrival in South America and hoped we felt welcome. He continued to surprise me.

We met the masters at a hotel then we took a bus deeper into the Sacred Valley to Urubamba. However, before leaving the hotel, Kamaq Wageaq pulled me aside, with the translator and urgently spoke to me. What he said surprised me and I didn't know what to do with the information, so I filed it away and said nothing. He told me that he had a message for me from Ille Tecsi Wiracocha and he was very sorry but I was responsible for the awakening of Africa. I must have looked shocked because the master repeated again that he was sorry. I had no idea what he was talking about. Awakening Africa? How? Bringing awareness of the Andean Tradition? I simply did not understand and he did not explain further.

We traveled to Urubamba, our base for the next ten days. We stayed at an old monastery, converted into a hotel. The accommodation was simple, the environment breathtaking with the Andes rising up around us. At one point the hotel was unable to supply water to the rooms due to a mechanical problem with the pump and for three days we did not shower or bath, while a part was being sourced. It was a very different experience from the one I was accustomed to, and truthfully I loved it. The simplicity of it all brought to me a purity of connection to nature, which was spellbinding.

A small group of us decided to spend a day visiting a sacred site not far from Urubamba – Ollyantaitambo – the seat of the warriors in the Inka Empire. It was there that I was to have a powerful and magical experience which has stayed with me clearly over the years.

We climbed to the top of this spectacular ruin and I stood on the topmost steps gasping for air. The altitude was very high and the climb gruelling and endless. Ollyantaitambo is gracefully positioned at the top of what feels like, a thousand step stairway, several hundred feet above the ground nestled into the mountainside. Beautiful rock terraced to perfection spread above me. I had reached the lower terraces of the temple area.

To my left were amazing, shaped rocks with square protrusions small enough to cup in my hands, paired at various intervals. I had no idea as to their use but they fascinated me, so I moved towards them. I pressed my body against the rock and breathed deeply. The energy was very powerful. My body began to vibrate gently – I looked down, my legs were actually shaking with the vibration. I was used to feeling energy but not like this!

Suddenly I felt I was being watched, I felt a presence behind me and to my right. Slowly I turned around, and there stood a beautiful husky dog.

I was surprised to see him, I had expected a human. He stood with his front paws resting on a small boulder and his back legs on the ground. He watched me with ice blue eyes, wagging his tail and smiling. He was gorgeous. 'A young teenager' I thought and smiled back. I moved over to him. He barked playfully and allowed me to stroke his soft fur, touch his face and cuddle his ears. I was in love.

We playfully interacted for a while, and then as suddenly as he arrived, he left, bounding off around an outcrop on the path to the next terrace. I sighed with gratitude returning to my rock, hoping to continue my vibrating experience.

I had settled against a giant boulder when I heard the most terrible sound - screaming. My body was instantly a knot, my heart froze, my solar plexus shut down and I felt terror sweep through my body. The sound was shocking. I ran towards it. It came from the path leading to the upper terraces.

I had no idea where the strength and the power that enabled me to move so fast came from. I just had to get to the source of that sound.

I came around the corner and there; my dog lay still, but the sound continued. I thought it was screaming, but he was howling because dogs don't scream, do they?

My instinct was to stop this beautiful creatures' pain, so I put my hands out, touching him gently, and miraculously he stopped screaming. My heart swelled with love and I beseeched spirit to help this creature. Suddenly I heard a powerful gentle voice say "We are assessing your consciousness". I felt the essence and power within this animal. I did not understand. I continued to administer energy and love – healing – to my new found friend who had captured my heart in the instant he had penetrated my space with his piercing gaze.

A young Spanish man arrived on the scene, maybe minutes later but for me time was suspended, with a sense of the unreal as I knelt on the rock. More people came, someone said the dog belonged to the young Spanish man who worked at the ruins, and the dog had fallen from the ledge above onto the path. I looked up – a drop of at least twenty-five feet onto hard rock. "Please help this creature, this beautiful creation, please help him" My heart beseeched.

A young woman was there, someone said she was a vet; she was checking bones and stated that the back legs were damaged.

When I heard her words I felt a strong resistance build in me, I knew she was wrong. I kept pouring energy into the furry soft playful being. I bit back tears, feeling my will surge to the surface. She was wrong.

A few minutes of eternity passed, people spoke around me, I was oblivious. The same gentle powerful voice spoke again – instructing me to walk the path to the ledge from where the dog had fallen. I was compelled. I was then told to call the dog.

I didn't know his name so I just called him, making dog calling sounds. He lifted his head, looked up at me, hesitated and then sprang up and bounded to me. He didn't even limp and my heart shone. My gratitude was boundless.

When we returned to the monastery that night I told Kamaq Wageaq through the translator, of my experience and he said that I had been assessed and blessed by the warriors of Ollyantaitambo.

There were six other initiates with me that day and we all had cameras. They all took pictures, at my insistence, of 'my' dog and I. Weeks later and back home, they told me one by one that the pictures had not come out. One lady had still not developed her pictures. I prayed and asked Spirit to give me just one photo. I have it still.

I have subsequently traveled many times to Peru and also Ollyantaitambo, which remains for me a very powerful and sacred place. I have had further communications and blessings from the keepers of Ollyantaitambo and feel a sense of belonging, of being home. Most of the initiates who visit this special country have the same sense.

"One of my most profound memories is my third level initiation in Peru. Before I left for Peru I felt nostalgic for a country I never seen before. This place haunted my dreams and meditations.

I had dreams of walking the streets of Cusco. In my meditations I saw mountains with trees and bushes and a river in the valley. When I arrived in Cuzco I was disappointed, the mountains had no trees or bushes, and they were bald. I wondered what mountains I had seen in my meditations. Later I went to Machu Picchu. These were the mountains from my meditations.

The energies in Peru affected me. They were so familiar, and easy to be in. The mountains talked to me, I saw their faces and I knew them, knew their mood if they were happy, angry or serious.

I saw faces on every stone I picked up, most clearly those that I took from the places of initiation. I knew that those places and stones would teach me, sharing wisdom and I have not been disappointed. The whole experience touched me on an entirely different level, one I do not access in my daily reality." - Ania

CHAPTER NINE

THE SHADOW AND INITIATION

ALLYU ALTO MISAYOQ

A day later I underwent my *Ayllu Altomisayoq* level of initiation. This is the third level in the Andean Tradition and in the words of the masters, "It is the beginning of mastery". This is perhaps a good time to look a little deeper into initiation.

In the West we tend to apply a lot of ego to the word 'master'. It comes with connotations of dominance and superiority. My understanding and experience are now different to my initial perception.

In the Andean Tradition when we refer to a master we refer to a level of consciousness and energy mastery. Everything is made up of energy. This understanding has lived through many generations of indigenous people in the Andes; a rural simple people living in harmony with nature, navigating by the stars, living from the land. It is only in recent years in the modern world that science and physics confirm this ancient belief as a reality. With this understanding, we also recognize that what lives has consciousness and can be communicated or interacted with.

Mastery is first mastery of self, the capacity and consciousness to manage the various energies which make up our being, our nature – the conscious management of our bodies, minds, sentiments and emotions. To this end the four elements are a loving and powerful tool. As explained when we discussed the elements, we use earth to balance our physicality, water our sentimental feelings, air our minds and fire to balance our strong emotions.

Next we are able to begin mastery of our environment. This should not be mistaken for dominance of any kind and is always motivated by the desire to be of service to humanity and the *Pachamama*. Our environment is governed by the laws of the universe, also present in nature. They create harmony rather than imbalance. With consciousness in our interactions with the environment and the subsequent support of nature, we are able to flow with these laws and experience ourselves and our lives as a part of the *Pachamama*. When we function outside of this natural flow we create stress and become reactive. For example when we need to make change in our lives, change that would support our growth like seasons changing, we can through fear and attachment, resist this natural flow and cause ourselves stress.

At this level of consciousness it becomes possible to manage energies relating to others too. This is the act of service, to help transform and transmute difficulties, blockages and wounds for our brothers and sisters. We begin to work with the various levels of group consciousness, which carry within them limiting beliefs and destructive patterning. Through understanding these beliefs and patterns we are able to transcend them and access our own liberation. Once liberation and transcendence is achieved, managing these consciousnesses is also possible.

The true initiation schools all offer tools for energy management. This management is vital to save or preserve energy, and not waste it on self-indulging patterns, attachment and control of areas of our lives which are transitional at best. Saving and preserving our energies is necessary to reach the greater levels of consciousness, the dimensions of light and awareness beyond the third dimensional reality. These dimensions exist as a constant state, but humans waste so much energy on the mundane that it feels impossible to access them. When we harness and preserve our energies, directing them with clear intent, these other dimensions and worlds become an attainable domain. In the Andean tradition we call this mastery.

BECOMING HUMAN

An important part of this process is transcending our own humanness. For myself and many others, I have seen how hard it is to accept our shadow aspects. These are the parts that we don't like and would rather pretend don't exist. And yet in us all, they do. It is the shadow, the polarity, of our light. For many years I pretended these aspects of me did not exist and unwittingly tried to bypass them. In that state they were barely acknowledged, never managed, and they tend to rise up at inopportune moments, offering a reflection I found shameful.

Kamaq Wageag told me it was not possible to transcend the human consciousness by detouring around it. I needed to travel through it in order to arrive where I wanted to be. I needed to embrace my human self, with all the aspects that I either didn't like or perceived as being imperfect and weak. He explained that it was only by coming to accept if not actually loving this part of myself that I could move beyond it. In this way I would finally be able to express myself naturally and fearlessly, realizing my full potential. To do this I faced my shadow, coming to understand the reason for its existence and finally arriving at a deep compassion and acceptance of it. It was a long and interesting journey, at times difficult. However, I now feel more at peace with the human aspects of myself and although my shadow is still alive and, at times kicking, it is something I can manage in myself without projecting it at others and causing undue harm.

The 'shadow' journey is triggered and experienced within the greater journey through initiation. Many ancient cultures on our beloved planet contained the same process of initiation and accelerated evolution. Sadly the oral transmissions of wisdom and the accompanying energy transmissions have been largely lost to us today. These cultures are either legends or are damaged beyond repair. In Africa the Bushman culture carried the initiation process and its transmissions were given in the living word, but this culture has all but been obliterated. In Central America the Mayan culture met with a similar fate, as did too the Natives of North America and the Aboriginals of Australia. As the modern world has influenced and invaded more regions these cultures have been sacrificed. In certain cases we can still access some of the transmissions of energy and knowledge, thanks to the masters who broke the silence of their ancestors, thus leaving information to enable us to live in harmony with planet Earth and her inhabitants.

At first glance there are aspects of the Andean Tradition, associated with Shamanism. They include practices with the four elements, the nature spirits, and mountain spirits called *Apus*. As I journeyed deeper with this tradition however, I understood it is also associated with the ancient wisdom schools that originated thousands of years ago. Many operated in secrecy and practiced underground, amidst mystery and rumors and these included the Rosicrucian, Essene and the Cathar orders. Prior to 1200 AD the mystery schools and various religions co-existed and influenced each other peacefully. From the reign of Pope Innocence III the persecution of several deeply spiritual groups, including the Cathars and the Templers began. This Crusade forced the mystery schools to operate in secrecy and spanned hundreds of years.

Our Greek ancestors believed, as their mythology proves, that the planets were living consciousness. Their mythology also reflects the process of 'death and rebirth' a theme common to initiation practices in all ancient wisdom schools. This theme perpetuates in the initiation processes of the Andean Tradition, with death of old consciousness and rebirth of new and more powerful ones. The Andean Tradition is an interesting and powerful continuation of this spirituality.

Most shamanic traditions use certain hallucinogenic plants to achieve altered states of consciousness. In the Amazonian tradition, Ayahuasca is used regularly and in Central America - Peyoti. The Andean Tradition has no need of these plants, as it is through the natural expansion of consciousness and conscious energy management that dynamic states of being and perceiving are accessed. Coca is however used expansively in the Andean Tradition. It has no hallucinogenic effect but produces a subtle energy to assist the Andean priest with connection. This plant is sacred in the Andean Tradition but is unnecessary for connection. Several power plants are experienced once only during the fourth level initiation, to gain understanding and experience of practices of masters in other traditions, and humbly, to participate in their ceremonies.

The Andean Tradition and the Inca Empire are directly associated, although the Andean Tradition dates back around 16 000 years to the Caral valley of the central Peruvian coast and the Inca Empire is dated less than 1 000 years ago. Legend tells us Manco Capac, the original *Inca* (*Inca* was a title given to the male leader, and there was only one at any given time) and *Mama Oclla* (the *Q'olla* – the female partner to the Inca) rose from the waters of Lake Titicaca on a golden disk. They went on to found one of the greatest empires our world has seen. It spanned an area greater than that of Alexander the Great and spread through what is now five different countries, in South America – Peru, Bolivia, Columbia, Ecuador and Argentina.

During their reign and their subsequent lineage, they incorporated many diverse cultures and tribes into the Empire. They took the best of each tribe and made it a part of the emerging culture. For example if a tribe excelled at weaving, they then would become the master weavers and would lead this area of the Empire. These areas and tribes were originally shamanic and it appears it is from this influence that the tradition incorporated the use of the elements, and nature to bring about the balance which each individual must access to evolve.

The Sacred Andean tradition tells another legend that the knowledge of the *Inka* culture originates from the land beneath the Atlantic Ocean where 102 *Inkas* made possible the manifestation of the *Imperial Tawantinsuyo* - four *suyos* or four directions.

The Andean Tradition offers initiation, and the core energy of the teachings remain still intact. I attribute this to its geographical location. In the Andes, where the tradition is still practiced and followed by the indigenous people, the air is very thin and the terrain hard. When the Spanish Conquistadors invaded many locals fled into the mountains and the high jungles. The Spanish were simply not equipped to follow at those altitudes, and so the Andean tradition went unchanged.

Initiation brings energy movement in a dual fashion. There is an expansion of one's consciousness outwards and a movement of one's awareness inwards. The senses are heightened, not temporarily, nor in a hallucinogenic way, but subtly and permanently. The individuals' perceptions shift and reality starts to appear different. This deeper awareness is applied with integrity and responsibility to both the external and internal worlds.

The movement inwards provides an opportunity for self-examination, looking at what we are and discarding what we are not. This enables recognition of conditioning and its patterning and movement beyond it. To be ourselves in spite of what we have been taught we should be. There is also a transcendence of ego as we discard fear, defensiveness and insecurity. This enables us to identify who we really are and not our appearance, what we do for a living, nor our intellectuality and our possessions.

The outward expansion of consciousness brings a shift in perception, enabling us to go beyond limiting beliefs. It shows us new levels of truth and deeper understanding of self, humanity and the human / spirit experience. It takes us beyond illusion and the archetypal energies.

"Prior to my journey in the Andean Tradition I had trained in several energy disciplines. I knew about energy and I had felt it but I did not trust the information I received. I analyzed and intellectualized my experiences.

After my first initiation my experience changed totally. It was an eye opener to face myself and my reality in a meaningful way. Before, I knew about energy, now I was dealing with it directly and experiencing it. Prior to initiation I knew I carried certain patterns and issues but I had never been beyond them, whereas after initiation I moved through them and quickly. For example I can be very stubborn; after initiation this manifested itself in my knees and demanded intervention. On confronting myself, it cleared and I was able to move beyond it." - Herbert

Many years ago I received a message from the Pachamama. She said, "The external world takes its reflections from our own internal perceptions". When undergoing the initiation journey, responsibility becomes essential. To understand our relationship with all else, we must first look at our relationship with ourselves.

These energetic movements span months, if not years, depending on the individual, their level of consciousness and the stage of initiation.

The initiation process creates change in the internal relationship with self and perhaps more importantly, creates a direct connection with the divine forces of light.

As we journey forward towards this light, we must clear and heal the imbalances within ourselves. These imbalances affect our perceptions, our emotions, our actions, our choices, and are often rooted in our patterning and conditioning. As we start healing our imbalances, so the inner truthful nature is revealed. This is the part of us that is our essence and our Divinity.

In the Andean Tradition, it is said, 'in order to know who we are we must look through the eyes in the back of heads to the past.' At first this sounded odd, however now I understand and value its wisdom. It means we must clear all the wounds and patterns of the past in order to experience our truth.

As we evolve our healing reveals our connection to the universe, the powers that govern it and their manifestation. The natural order and flow of life become aligned and our lives and our expression flow freely. It is possible to be completely comfortable with who we are in acceptance of reality as it presents itself, and fully in service of Divine Will.

INITIATION LEVELS

There are various levels of initiation in the Ancient Andean Tradition. Each level carries a title and brings specific inner growth and balance, enabling a different level of understanding of reality.

Pacqo

The first Initiation is the Pacqo level. This is the level of the Spiritual Seeker and it is the beginning. We are birthed into our power and begin a very personal relationship with the four elements of earth, air, fire and water, and their reflections within us. We begin to understand nature and the nature of being human.

Pampa Misayoq

The second Initiation is the Pampa Misayoq. In the second initiation discipline and humility are established and there is a great expansion of our intuitive energies. The emphasis is on service to our community and humanity. We are able to perform ceremony at this level but it is offered to *Ille Tecsi Wiracocha* through one of the elements and the *Apus* (mountain energies). We learn the cosmological order of the *Despacho*, and the direct connection with the energy of Coca leaves, and their domain.

The third Initiation or the *Alto Misayoq* initiation has three stages to it, each given as a separate initiation.

Ayllu Alto Misayoq:

This initiation is undertaken in Peru. With permission of the Andes Mountains – *Apus* - we are given the authority to access healing power. This power also enables the initiate to better master their own energies. This initiation is incorporation and consecration into the sacred energies of the Andes and the result is a greater connection to our personal power. This is the beginning of the journey into self-mastery.

Llagta Alto Misayoq

The second stage of the third level is known as the *Llagta Alto Misayoq* initiation. It is the experience of relinquishing everything that no longer serves us. It is a journey through the shadow, darkness of our own nature, and transcending this to find our own internal light. The understanding of healing is further given, working with many different natural elements to heal self and others. The priest is empowered to perform ceremony, which is sent to and received directly by *Ille Tecsi Wiracocha*.

Suyu Alto Misayoq:

This is the final stage of third level and having faced and accepted our humanness we are offered the opportunity to go beyond it, opening to the experience of several dimensions simultaneously. We are now operating at a level of global consciousness, and have the knowledge and understanding of all that exists and all manifested life in totality and clarity.

Kuraq Akulleq:

This is the final stage of initiation available at this time. There are a total of seven levels prophesized for the future. This initiation brings the full acceptance of self, the acknowledgement of our own mastery, both within our own tradition and in universal knowledge. We no longer work with the Earth *Apus* but with guidance from the stars. This guide is called *Itu*. A priest at this level can heal people in a ritualistic way and should be able to manage planetary and solar consciousness.

Through each initiation, tools and methods in healing, divination and energy management are taught. It is through the use and experience of these tools and methods that, over time, infinite understanding and empowerment are reached.

There is an extraordinary tangible relationship with Spirit formed for the initiate, a relationship manifesting through the three worlds, bringing comfort protection and guidance as the initiate needs it. The forms it may take and the ways in which it will manifest are indeed mysterious.

Often a person is 'called' to the path of initiation by Spirit.

Kamaq Wageag, my master, was driving in a snow storm and stopped, attempting to clean the wind screen of his car, he leant out the driver's window. Lightning struck in the area, and moved through the metal of the vehicle and into him. He lost consciousness. A while later, when he regained consciousness he found his clothes smoking, his eyebrows, eyelashes and hair badly singed and his senses in turmoil. He was unable to hear and saw only the colour orange. For three days afterwards he couldn't sleep. Being struck by lightning is a traditional form of calling to Shamanism, across many cultures where lightning is a natural phenomenon, not only the Andean tradition.

My own calling came through illness. The way in which Spirit will reach us is as individual as we are.

"When in Peru undertaking my third level initiation, I received a very clear message from Apu Chicon telling me to follow one path only. It made sense to me because while I had been initiating in the Andean Tradition I had also been studying the Kabala and working with the Angels. Even though I understood the message I did not know which path to choose.

On return to South Africa I asked for guidance and in response Archangel Raphael came to me in a meditation and told me to follow the star path. I did not understand this message. Nor did I understand which path was the path of the stars but thought that with time it would reveal itself. In a later contact with Raphael I saw two men at an airport with a third person. I identified the two men as the Andean masters but was confused who the third person was, but knew he was the one who would bring the star path.

A few months later I was talking to another initiate in the Andean Tradition and he mentioned that at the fourth level of initiation the initiate is no longer guided by the Apus but by Itu – a star. I went cold and told him the story of my dilemma. It all fell into place and I knew that the Andean Tradition was the path of the Stars. I later pieced together the origins of the tradition to the Pleiades via Mars and Venus. I finally understood." - Richard

Future initiations were prophesized, which will earth and reveal new levels of consciousness in years to come.

Sapa Inca:

The *Sapa Inka* will have so much energy that their auric body will be luminous day and night to the observer. They will heal bodies, and the consciousness of humanity. This priest will have the capacity to drive the will and love of humanity as a group.

Malku Inca:

A priest at this level will heal simply through a touch of their hand. This priest will be able to re-order and re-balance the physical body, the minds and will of people.

Taytanchis:

The final level of initiation that will be made available on our beautiful planet is the *Taytanchis*. This being will reign in the world in absolute love. It is said that this is the manifestation of God consciousness on our planet and our conduit to the realm of our Creator and that plain of consciousness.

It is not a particular person who will attain these levels, living them as an example to others as with many of the great Masters in the past. Rather it will be grounded by an individual or several simultaneously, and then become generally available to those who seek it for themselves. At this level of consciousness there is no abuse of power so the desire to rule over others will not exist; there is only a desire to elevate the level of consciousness of the entire planet.

CHAPTER TEN

APUS & COCA

The time in Peru was astounding and at the end of it, I was grateful I did not have a lot of time left for sightseeing. I needed to come home to assimilate and integrate what I had experienced.

The third level initiation was an incredible journey through the sacred sites of the Andes and the Sacred Valley in Peru. Although there were new teachings, this initiation was more experiential, with being initiated into the energies of these ancient and sacred places.

We spent several days in close interaction with our masters. Time did not diminish my high perceptions of them; but it had made them seem more accessible and more human. The spiritual love and light they generated constantly, coupled with the new human perceptions I had of them, served to highlight their individual specialness. I actually wept when I said goodbye to them, feeling I was moving beyond the warmth of safety that was home. I wept also when I left Peru, a country that had captured my heart.

I had received my ceremonial clothing during this initiation, which included a poncho made from Llama wool that had been hand woven generations before, a *Chullo* - a colorful woven woolen cap complete with ear flaps and pompoms; a *Chumpi* - a broad woven woolen belt worn to cover the naval and a *Chuspa* - a small woven bag hung around the neck. This clothing is worn when performing ceremonies and rituals. However, when simply teaching or instructing the *Chumpi* alone will suffice. The fabric is beautiful made from bright colorful weaves of ancient symbols, the four elements and symbols from daily living. Many of the items are not new but are used antiques, owned for generations within families and tribes but eventually sold off in the markets. The colors spoke to me instantly, their vibrancy reflected in their energy.

All these items are traditional, and are worn by *Alto Misayoqs* with a sense of honor and sacredness. They are also made for life in the Andes where snow, ice and biting wind is a daily occurrence. Therefore they are not only items of ceremony but are also practical. As the kit is not designed for the heat and sun of Africa, it is used purely for ceremonial purposes here.

All the initiates are given their Quechua names at this initiation (Quechua is the language spoken by the great majority of the indigenous people of Peru). The Quechua name is a reflection of the energy of the person, and embodies their path, their attitudes and their nature. My name was given as *Kanchay Anqa,* which means the Warrior of Light. Being renamed in this way was an interesting experience as we each came to embody the name we had been given, or perhaps recognized its qualities within us.

"I was in The Temple of The Moon, on the seat of the Moon, and in meditation. I stretched my arms forward sending all my prayers to Ille Tecsi Wiracocha and as I retracted them, I felt myself receiving the blessings of the Divine. And then it happened.

The energies of Ille Tecsi Wiracocha struck me. What a feeling and what a surprise. I didn't know something like that was possible. And then I heard Kamaq Wageaq saying, "YES". He had seen it.

Later I received my Quechua name 'Kanchay Illapa', The Ray of Light. I believe it is from my experience at the Seat of the Moon that my name is derived. The whole experience was beautiful. I will never forget it. Thank you, master." - Ania

APU

During this initiation there is a personal introduction to the *Apu*, the spirits of the mountains. The *Apus* are explained as a part of the teachings initially, but this introduction is of an energetic nature. The Alto Misayoq begins to establish a conscious relationship with a particular *Apu* and receives guidance on their path from the Spirit of this mountain. The *Apu* is the highest expression of the Earth energy and has power and influence over vast areas of their continent and all living things or all life within their surface radius. They are a part of the earth but are of individual consciousness, either male or female.

In the Andean Tradition we acknowledge the *Kawsay* or living energy in all forms of life. From the biological systems of our human body, to the nature in our environment, everything that lives is based on and moves through energy. The entire planet is interconnected through channels of energy called *Secques* and in each *Secque* there are several *Apus* or centers of planetary energy. This energy influences life in this area or continent. Their energy is either *Yanantin* or *Masantin*, male or female. The *Secques* are similar to the channels of energy found in the human anatomy, in Chinese medicine called *Meridians* or *Nadis* in the *Ayurvedic* system of healing.

Through this grid or lattice work of veins of energy, and through our consciousness we can access these *Secques*. Through the *Secques* we can access the planetary subconscious and the various layers of consciousness associated with different towns, regions, and cultures. In this way we are able to access the consciousness of the Apus, the spirits of the mountains. Through the journey of initiation we access these forms of consciousness and integrate them into our own, growing ourselves into deeper and higher states of priesthood.

The relationship to the *Apus* was to become a very important and supportive one. The *Apus* act as physical Earth guides to us, and once conscious connection is made they can assist us in many ways.

Through them I have received safe passage on journeys into other places, found things I presumed lost, been guided to areas or places of practical importance, been fed energy of various types when I have needed them, received guidance as to the management of various situations and circumstances and have been held and comforted when I have had need. Their consciousness and presence is very real and I have never been denied help.

It is necessary from time to time to offer gratitude, through ceremonial offering, so that *Ayni* is present in the relationship. There is no specific timing for this, and although the *Apus* are acknowledged and honored in every *Despacho* ceremony performed, some additional personal gratitude never goes amiss.

A friend planned to climb Kilimanjaro in Africa. At the time she had gone through a major life change; she had given up smoking, begun a new more physical lifestyle. I understood that this climb was very important for her and if she got this right she would feel powerful enough to surmount anything.

I performed a ceremony, a *Despacho* for her and those climbing with her. Before she left I told her that she should take a small stone from the mountain, with its permission, and place this in her right pocket. This was a trick *Hatun Runa* had shown me and it granted the power of the mountain as stamina, vitality and focus. I used it many times in Peru where the altitude can be an impediment for the unaccustomed, especially when hiking. It worked.

My friend climbed with her exhausted group. Feeling exhilarated and not at all tired, she kept looking at and commenting on the landscape until she realized the others were becoming irritated with her. They were exhausted and focused on finishing, whilst she was chatting and strongly strolling along. At some point she reached into her pocket and found a stone, but had no recollection of putting it there. She asked her hiking companion if he recalled it. He responded in the negative, but there it was. Her connection with Kilimanjaro effected subsequent life changes, growing and expanding her in many ways.

There are many legends and stories of the *Apus*, how they are able to take on form, presenting themselves as people. It is said that they do this to test us, checking our consciousness, our generosity and our faith. These stories have a similar theme, telling of people visited by the *Apus* as travelers or homeless lost individuals who request help. If help is given there is reciprocation, a gift from the *Apus*, sometimes physical but always a blessing in abundance and support, *Ayni*.

When I travel to a new place, flying or driving, I make a point of greeting the *Apus* of that place and asking permission to be there. I find that it brings flow to my journey providing what I need easily, sometimes before I know that it is needed.

On and off for two years a colleague and friend, Madlen and I traipsed through the Magaliesburg looking for a specific type of venue where we could host the Andean workshop in South Africa. We had a venue that we had used for years, but a change was necessary. We had visited so many but always our requirements were not totally met. One day as we were leaving yet another unsuitable venue, in desperation I said out loud, "*Apus*, please show us a place where people can be introduced to the *Pachamama* and the Andean Tradition". A moment later, the sensation that we needed to turn down a road we had just passed became overwhelming and I told Madlen to turn the car around and go back there. Sure enough there was a venue and it had everything we would need for our workshop and more.

In the Andean Tradition it is not only the *Apus* that are acknowledged as living consciousness, but the plants, rocks and animals too. Everything that has a natural frequency has consciousness, and through the expansion of our own consciousness we are able to tap into these other forms and communicate with them. It is not a bizarre experience but a natural, gentle communion beyond our material selves with the living universe.

"As my vibration changes and grows my perception of the Apus changes. The depth and clarity of my communication with them increases. After visiting the Andes on my third level initiation, in meditation, I perceived the Spirit of Chicon. I saw the physical mountain as white, I glimpsed a face, and there was light coming from, and pouring into the top of the Apu. This light traveled through the sky as a great beam, connecting to the stars. Now I call the Apus to me when I administer healing and I feel their presence. They impart information about the person and their problems, which helps effect better results". - Richard

COCA

In the Incan Empire two items were held sacred above all others, Gold and Coca. Gold was perceived as being the yellow metal of *Inti* the sun, with no trade or commercial value. It was consecrated for *Inti*. Coca was perceived as a sacred plant with magical powers, and enabled direct connection to *Inti*.

In the Andean Tradition Coca is treated with absolute respect and sacredness. In ceremony it is used as a carrier of our intentions and wishes to the *Hanaq Pacha*.

In Peru the presence of Coca is constant. It has many physical and nutritional values and is used by Peruvians and visitors alike to assist with altitude sickness, inflammations, blood circulation and pressure, headaches, digestive complaints, water retention, dental complaints and dizziness among other things.

Coca contains more than 600 vitamins, minerals and amino acids. It is possible to sustain the body for prolonged periods on Coca and water alone. It is also an appetite suppressant and increases vitality and, in centuries past, was given by land-owners to their laborers instead of food.

The leaves can be steeped in hot water and used as a '*matte*' tea, or 'chewed'. The leaves are rolled around in the mouth to moisten them, and then tucked between the gum and the cheek. In ceremony the Coca is used by the priest in this way to create connection between the third eye *nawi* (chakra) and the throat *nawi*. Coca acts as a carrier of energies and assists the priest to access higher vibrations and to verbalize or externalize them. Many other herbs require other additives to extract their goodness, but Coca can simply be used in its natural form for optimal benefit.

Coca is only used orally by the priest during ceremony but is given to the participants as a vehicle and connection for their intentions. They do not use the Coca orally, but hold the leaves over the third eye, imprinting their intentions into it. The priest includes these Coca leaves in the ceremony.

Initiation teaches the use of Coca as a tool for divination. Each leaf is treated like a Tarot card or Rune, representing a certain message or indicating a symbol, depending on its shape, color and size.

Like everything in this dimension, Coca has shadow energy too. It was prophesized by the *Inka Pachacuti* humanity would destroy the sacredness of the Coca by abusing its light. Coca is the plant from which Cocaine is manufactured. Its shadow is as powerful as its light. Cocaine is highly addictive and deeply destructive on many levels to the human psyche. Its shadow will stimulate and arouse the shadow of the user quickly. Coca in its natural state has no hallucinogenic properties; its most significant effect in ceremony is to assist with connection and centeredness.

Today in Peru there are 682 official Coca farms, and more than twenty million people in the Andes use Coca as a dietary supplement, for medicinal purposes and in the ceremonies.

"We were in the African bush miles away from any town. I was unable to sleep, my breathing was labored as my chest tightened and I experienced much discomfort in my lungs. I worried that I was becoming sick, and that I couldn't afford to as we were far from medical assistance and the maintenance of the camp depended on me. After a few days of this it occurred to me to perform a ceremony for my well-being. All I had at my disposal was Coca and red wine. I made an offering of these two elements to the Earth. Also immediately the pressure and discomfort in my chest released and sleep returned to me." - Herbert

SYMBOLS

Another powerful tool in the Andean Tradition is the use of symbols. In many spiritual traditions the world over, the use of symbols, varying in shape, design and meaning is an ancient and common practice. They are usually geometric forms, which when utilized with intention, carry a frequency or connect the user to a frequency. Whether it is because the inherent shape and design are keys to particular energies or whether these symbols carry the intention of generations of users over thousands of years, they do enable access to energies for specific purposes. In the Andean Tradition we use symbols for protection, clearing blockage, drawing spiritual power, among other things. At certain levels of initiation these tools are taught to compliment what is being accessed and stimulated within the initiate.

"We were 'importing' a male lion from one an African national parks to another in the same country, as companion to the last remaining female lion in that region. Her pride had been wiped out by poachers and we hoped she would accept the new male and together they would breed.

There was a lot of difficulty in making the arrangements, and as the weeks dragged on with no movement I felt despondent. I had to do something so I decided to send energy to the situation through symbols.

Eventually permission was granted and all the necessary permits and paper work were underway. Our boy was on his way." - Herbert

Symbols give direction to our intentions, and the greater the power of the user the more effective the results.

"When filming in the wild, we are at risk from the wild animals in the bush. Often elephants ambled towards us and it was scary.

Desperately, on one such occasion and without thinking, I visualized symbols and sent them to the elephants with the intention they move off in another direction. It worked beautifully. I have also found it most effective with other animal species." - Herbert

CHAPTER ELEVEN

BABA CREDO AND THE AFRICAN TRADITIONS

After my third level initiation, I returned to South Africa to re-embrace my life. After initiation there is a period of adjustment and although I was able, over time, to settle back into my physical reality, the perceptions, understanding and relationship with my world was never the same again. Fundamental change takes place, deepening and expanding.

I had established over the previous year a healing centre where a number of other therapists worked, including me. It was a dream I had for many years, and through effort and hard work I had established it. On return from that initiation I realized I loathed it. I was no longer a healer; I was a business manager with responsibilities that had become burdens. Not only were clients and patients depending on me but the therapists were looking to me to provide them with work. I felt myself sinking under the strain.

I realized that I did not need this healing centre, the only thing I needed as a healer where my hands and my intention. It did not matter if I worked under a tree or under a roof. My passion was being swamped by the gift-wrap in which I had packaged myself, and my work. I gave everyone enough notice and shut it down.

At the same time, Spirit asked me to take a great leap in faith. I had worked in healing for many years and had a very busy practice. It was self-supporting and while this was my passion, it was also my source of income. One day during a treatment I heard a very clear message that I needed to stop healing. I asked what I was supposed to do in its place and I was told channeling. By this stage I was talking to Spirit non-stop. Most clients booked for healings but it was the messages they wanted, and I often found myself distracted from healing by the stream of communication between client and Spirit. So I sent a message to all my clients letting them know I would no longer be practicing as a healer, and would now only be channeling. It was extraordinary. As a channel I continued to see seven or eight clients a day and there was no change in my income. The transition was amazing.

These changes may seem to have been undertaken rashly, but I have learnt that if I make a decision and don't act on it immediately, fear, doubt and uncertainly begin to plague me. So when I feel sure of a choice initially I simply follow through. It is a method that is yet to prove incorrect for me.

I did realize two important things. Firstly, I identified with the role of healer and I questioned for weeks, "If I am not a healer then who am I?" It was a good question and was followed by a good lesson. I never again identified myself with a role or archetype in such a fixed way. My sense of self has come from who I am and not from what I do or what I have. Secondly, I had been aware of the other therapists' dependency on me but the dependency of my clients had slipped my notice. Most were not taking responsibility for their own well-being or growth. They came for healing and felt good for a while, but they would not follow through on the advice being offered by Spirit. They would continue in the same patterns, and when those patterns became uncomfortable, they would book another healing. They were hiding from themselves and I was supporting it. I felt awful I had not noticed and had not acted in their highest good. These realizations made the transition feel right for all concerned.

I continued as a channel, operating from a small room in my home. I needed nothing more, and I felt hugely empowered.

BABA CREDO, ANIMAL TOTEMS AND CHANNELING

Several weeks before my first visit to Peru I had a series of disturbing experiences. They happened in the state before sleep, when we are still sufficiently aware to know that we are not dreaming but it is not happening in the solid physical reality either.

One night as I lay in bed waiting to curl up embraced in the void, I became aware of movement near my feet, and as I directed my awareness there I perceived a huge snake slithering up the bed towards me; it was thicker in girth than a beer drinking man and was very long, the gaping cavity of its mouth heading straight for me. I instinctively knew this snake wanted to swallow me. I have always had a generous fear of snakes and had no desire to be inside the belly of this one. I swore at it, using language I shall not repeat here and it vanished before my eyes. It took a while for me to relax enough to once again await the sweet embrace of sleep.

This same experience happened over and over in the weeks that followed; each night I would curse this apparition and it would vanish. I tried many things to avoid it, and occasionally managed but it returned, waiting for me. I was becoming progressively sleep deprived.

Finally the day came to leave for Peru and I thought I was leaving this nasty monster behind. But the first night I was settled into my bed in the hotel in Urubamba, there it was again. By then I had given this thought, overcoming my terror sufficiently to listen to my intuition. I was told to allow this snake to have its way with me! I was stunned but the vision was very persistent. So I did as was suggested. The experience was very real, I felt myself being absorbed into the gaping mouth of this monstrous snake and the blackness that followed became sleep. The vision did not return for the remainder of my Peru trip.

Some weeks later in South Africa I had another snake visitor. This one was smaller, but still a good two meters long with a girth as fat as a babies' fist. This 'little' chap was making his way up my body towards my mouth one night as I was falling asleep. I was able to maintain my intuition while this happened and I was told to open my mouth. This snake slithered its way down my throat. The sensations were very real but once I allowed the experiences to flow, I felt peaceful and safe.

Sometime after these experiences understanding came, brought by another extraordinary Master, the High *Sanusi* of Africa, Credo Vusamazulu Mutwa. Baba Credo, as he is affectionately called by the people of Africa, is a Sangoma or medicine man with the high wisdom and secret knowledge of his lineage and ancestors. He is one of the most powerful spiritual leaders and masters to emerge from Africa. A man who loves his people and Africa.

Before I gave up the healing centre, one night I had a dream. In my dream I lived in a house I do not own, and I was entertaining people I do not know. I walked into the kitchen, where a female domestic helper, whom I had never seen before, said to me, "Credo will see you now".

My dream puzzled me. The next morning I mentioned it to my client, Dina. "Credo Mutwa is calling you. You must go and see him" she said. I told Dina I had no idea how to go about arranging such a visit. She told me she knew how to put me in touch with Credo, and that she would make the arrangements for me. I felt a buzz of excitement, remembering my feelings when the Andean masters had met with him previously and thought, 'at last!'

Dina called to say it was arranged for two days later in the afternoon. I looked at my diary and groaned, I was booked to capacity and saw no way of changing things, but by the end of the day things had changed themselves. I had several cancellations for the afternoon in question and suddenly it was happening.

Two days later I drove out of the city with Dina to the mountains. Baba Credo, as I came to know him, lived with his wife Virginia in the Hennops river area, where the Magaliesberg mountain range begins. On arrival I felt withdrawn and nervous, and when Credo asked me why I was there I told him of my dream. He said the woman from my dream was his sister who had passed into Spirit many years before but who acted as a messenger for him. She had lived in Zimbabwe, and although a powerful *Sangoma* in her own right, she had worked as a domestic employee.

I didn't understand why I was there but Baba Credo accepted my presence and began to talk. He spoke of many things including Peru, which he had visited many times, Africa and the healing needed here. He also spoke about me. At the time it sounded like a conversation in riddles and I left dazed and confused, not understanding.

That night, as I was falling asleep I found myself back in his house, moving down the passage. Credo appeared in front of me and said, "So you have returned". I have no further recollection of this encounter but do not doubt its importance.

However, during our daytime visit he asked me if I knew what my totem animal was; I replied I thought it was the snake. He asked me why I thought that and I told him about being swallowed by the snake and I in turn swallowing it. He told me it was very rare for a white person to have the snake totem. Unfortunately I never questioned him on this remark and so to this day do not know why that is. He explained that being swallowed by the snake is to be absorbed by Spirit and to swallow the snake is an indication that Spirit is going to use your voice. Finally I understood what had happened. And shortly thereafter I had begun channeling. It made a lot of sense.

Credo gave me some advice on managing certain energies and ended by saying, "But who am I to tell a lion how to roar in her own den?" I know it may be obvious to you reading this but I did not see it until months later. My totem is the big cat.

In the Andean Tradition we do not work with totem animals per se. We honor the animals that govern or embody the qualities of the three worlds. The snake is the keeper of the *Uju Pacha* (world inside the Earth), the Puma (in South America) is the keeper of the *Kay Pacha* (our physical reality) and the Condor (again in South America) is the keeper of the *Hanaq Pacha* (upper realms of spirit). On other continents the Puma would be replaced by large felines i.e.: lions, tigers, jaguars and the condor would be replaced by large birds of prey i.e.: the eagle. The animal kingdom is honored as part of nature and is symbolized in all the ceremonies in the Andean Tradition.

SHAPE SHIFTING

There exists in all indigenous spiritual traditions the ability to 'shape shift'. This is often associated with the animal kingdom. Shape shifting describes the projection of one's consciousness into another life form in order to experience life as that form. In the Andean Tradition when we connect with a tree, we are able to project our consciousness in a way that connects us to the consciousness of that tree. If this connection is strengthened and deepened we are able to experience ourselves as that tree. More extreme examples of shape shifting involve animals.

In some shamanic traditions shape shifting is not always used only to access information and wisdom, it can be used negatively too. There are legends about certain shamans who are so well versed in shape shifting that they can use this tool to embody animals or even people. They do this by taking full control of the physical body of the 'shape' into which they are shifting. They do not alter their own form, nor join consciousness with another form but rather they possess another form. They dominate the will of the other form. There is a tribe of shamans in Bolivia who are famous for their possession of animals. This is a very dark practice as the shamans involved are said to commit atrocities while possessing the bodies of these animals.

This is a direct violation of the laws of the universe, the laws of nature and is not practiced in the Andean Tradition.

I speak often of consciousness and this might be a good time to explain my understanding and experience of it. Consciousness is an inner awareness with which we are all born. However, in most people it is under developed and not experienced as we operate primarily through thought. When we operate through thought we are influenced by the thought processes of others and the mental energies in our environments. This is because thought is a space outside of us and our own quiet internal truth. When we operate through thought our consciousness is not contained within us but is drawn outwards and exposed to many external factors, but primarily to our ego, the group consciousness or consensus realities. In this mental state our sense of self is no longer clear and so the use of intuition becomes difficult. We react emotionally to our thought processes and further our suffering.

The internal pathways or channels of energy within the human energy field connect us to Spirit and to our own Soul. Through these connections we have access to higher consciousness, Universal consciousness. When our consciousness is fed through our connection with Spirit through the internal pathways of energy, our intuition is better accessed. There is greater contentment and less influence from external factors. We are emotionally calmer and more discerning, as the conscious influence of our minds is calmer. We are better able to 'perceive' Spirits subtle guidance.

Once consciousness is accessed it can be directed through intention into any place or space that we choose. The mastery of our consciousness is a primary tool in the Andean Tradition. We use our consciousness to access other realms, dimensions and life forms. Shape shifting can be as simple as the projection of consciousness into a rock. Rocks have been around for millions of years, they have seen, felt, heard and experienced much. To access the consciousness of a rock is to access a source of enormous knowledge and wisdom.

CEREMONY OF PEACE

When the masters again visited South Africa I had the honor of visiting Baba Credo with them. I had no idea as to the purpose of the visit but I was in for a treat. Baba Credo and Virginia greeted us, Baba in his full ceremonial gear, looking spectacular. He wore a brass breast plate from which hung a dozen huge symbols sculpted in either brass or jade – I remember seeing an *ankh* (the Egyptian symbol of eternal life), and a huge jade heart, all suspended by thick hand hewn brass chains. He wore a brass helmet in the same style of craftsmanship. (At a later date he referred to this helmet as his 'gardening hat'). A pathway had been created with white candles from the garden into their reception room, also lit with candles. The sight was beautiful.

I was privileged to witness a ceremony performed between Credo and my teachers in which the candle of peace was lit between the continents of Africa and South America. This was a white candle in a simple brass holder, which had been hand made by Zulu women hundreds of years before. I felt I witnessed history in the making. I have subsequently learnt that when ceremonies of this nature were performed amongst the tribes of Africa in times past, peace would reign for hundreds of years, sometimes permanently. I felt deeply honored to witness the sacred in action.

I encountered Baba Credo several times in the astral state, sometimes with my masters, other times alone. On one occasion I felt his presence in my bedroom. I asked him why he was there and he said I was to receive a contract for Africa, but in order to receive it I must fall asleep. I asked questions regarding the contract, which were answered. He told me it was my destiny to take this contract on and fulfill it. I became aware of the masters in the room, and we also spoke a little. Baba Credo then reiterated that I must sleep. I lay there but was disturbed by the three of them chatting amongst themselves. I told them I could not sleep unless they were quiet. They laughed and then were silent. I slept but in the morning had no recollection of further events.

Through Baba Credos' wisdom I came to see similarities between the African traditions and the Andean tradition.

Years after these events I visited Baba Credo in Kuruman, a small town near the South African / Namibian border. He had moved there some years before. It saddened me to see this great man ageing and ailing but his spirit and wisdom was as powerful and enveloping as ever. He and Virginia have created a natural healing hospital for HIV and AIDS sufferers in the area. While showing us around his space, he pointed out several enormous boulders, used by them for healing. The boulders are placed in a circle with a large flat stone, large enough for an adult to lie on in the middle. He said these rocks had not been carried to this place but had been 'sung' there by him. My mind was immediately drawn back to the amazing structures I had seen in Peru, which even with our technology today we cannot recreate. I have heard theories about these structures being built through the power of sound. Baba Credo indicated his structure had been created in the same way.

He showed us a painting, which I have seen many times before in his home, a magnificent collage of symbols, meters long and at least a meter and a half wide. It is based on his prophetic dreams. In the right top corner are four women's faces. The first is of Queen Elizabeth II, followed by Winnie Madikizela Mandela, Indira Ghandi, the

Indian prime Minister who was assassinated. He said these women had all carried the tools to heal Africa but the first three had been side tracked in their mission and it amounted to nothing. He said that the final hope for Africa now lay with the fourth woman in the painting who would come to Africa holding the tools to heal Africa.

In the African traditions there is a deity, to whom homage is paid named *Wiracocha*. This Deity is associated with the sun. I found it fascinating that these two cultures, existing on different continents, separated by ocean, would share deity's attributed with similar qualities. Although in the Andean tradition *Ille Tecsi Wiracocha* is the Creator and in the African tradition the great Creator is *Nkulunkulu*.

In the African traditions, there is a way of community living called *Ubuntu*. It is similar to the Andean traditions *Ayni*, the law of reciprocity. Where giving for the sake of giving with no expectation of return is honored and excess is shared. In both traditions this excess is shared through entertaining the community. If an individual in the community has excess food after their household is fed they will host a community feast to share the excess.

Credo Mutwa has featured many times on my journey, and is an ongoing inspiration on my path. And although of another tradition, his wisdom, his understanding and his loving presence is an embodiment of the Mastery possible through the sacred path of initiation in the ancient indigenous traditions, all over the world. Through Baba Credo and my own beloved Masters I recognize this undefined presence of love as the true sign of a great Master.

My personal life was changing again. I was engaged, for a time. With the support I received from the three worlds and life - I was flourishing. I moved home and my practice, again. These changes happened so often I accepted them as a part of my journey but I did feel nomadic, and at times yearned to be in one place long enough to feel I had been there.

The community in South Africa grew fast and so did the responsibilities. Each year I arranged for new initiation groups to travel to Peru for the third level initiation. We performed monthly *Despachos,* also at equinoxes and solstices, and regularly offered meditation groups in different parts of the city.

Satellite communities sprung up in the Cape, Natal, Port Elizabeth and Nelspruit, and although each community had a manager, they were ultimately my responsibility. Two years past with another two annual workshops hosted in South Africa before I was invited to Peru for my next initiation.

The *Chakana* is the ancient cross of balance, the cross of the Inka Empire, the Empire of the *Tawantinsuyu* (discussed in more detail in chapter thirteen). It is held sacred in the Andean tradition, representing the principles and understanding of the tradition. It is usually carved from stone by Peruvian artisans, particularly those in the sacred valley of the Andes. On certain initiations we receive *Chakanas,* but also buy our own made from silver, stone, shell and even coral.

An event happened a few months before I left for Peru, seemingly inconsequential but for an experience that happened in Peru throwing a totally different light on it.

Corlia had purchased a Chakana in Peru previously, one half in black stone and the other in white stone. It had accidentally shattered, which upset her. A few weeks later the two of us were at my home. I had a similar Chakana, and felt the overwhelming urge to give it to her. She accepted the gift; it was a special warm, emotional moment for us both.

In Peru, I assisted on the third level initiation. Dusk was falling fast, the mountains blanketed in the deep indigo that precedes night. We were at Ollyantaitambo, and were finishing up for the day. We stood in the town square awaiting our transport back to Pisac and dinner. Suddenly out of the dusk a little girl, no older than ten years old, appeared. She stood in front of me with her hand fisted and arm outstretched. I extended my hand palm up to receive whatever was in her hand. I felt something prick my hand. My first thought was 'Oh lord, what is this? A strange insect perhaps? I immediately dropped what she had given me onto the cobbles, expecting it to scuttle away. In the gloom I peered down. It was a black and white Chakana exactly like the one I had given away.

I picked it up in amazement, glancing up to ask this girl why she was giving it to me, but she was gone, absorbed back into the indigo of dusk. I showed Hatun Runa. He responded that receiving it was not significant but that I had dropped it was. I looked at him puzzled as our transport arrived, thinking to myself, what is it with these Masters? Do they always have to speak in riddles?

Driving back to Pisac I sat silent, contemplating this experience. I tried to understand how a little girl in Peru could be connected to a Chakana I had given away weeks before in South Africa. There had been no one else in my home that day, and my friend from South Africa was not in Peru with me. I had told no one of that incident. So I accepted that the Apus or Pachamama had again honored me, witnessing my exchange weeks before and responding to my action. The masters' words puzzled me; what exactly did he mean?

CHAPTER TWELVE

DUALITIES

The initiation was powerful beyond imagination. It felt as though the previous initiations were a prelude. This initiation was both experiential and teachings, and dug deep into my psyche exposing so much of what was hidden. Some I would rather have left buried, but some was more manageable. The die was cast and the subsequent integration would become the journey of the warrior who slayed the dragon, emerging victorious but battle worn.

At a point over the three days of initiation we underwent a symbolic death which enabled me to regress, 'seeing' past lives, which had contributed to the wounding of my psyche and the subsequently created imbalances. I saw what had been done to me and also what I had done to others. It was startling. The lifetimes in which I experienced injustice were numerous and had certain themes – I was female and I accessed at the point of my death. These deaths were cruelly inflicted by men; drowning, beating, torturing, stabbing, shooting, strangulation, starvation. It was real but I did not suffer as

I recalled, rather I felt a sense of deep sadness that my executioners had moved so far from the truth that they had forgotten who they were – I wept, not for myself, but for them.

The sense of virtuousness was further imprinted when I looked at what I had done to others. One incident I remembered when I was at school in this life. I was cruel to a girl in my class because I did not like her. I felt horrendous about it and subsequently sent her so much light and healing that I am assured her life improved in all ways.

Persecution had resulted in these 'previous deaths' and my reactions in those lives didn't make sense of my feelings in this one. As I viewed the past lives I felt saddened for these people, and yet as I began my integration process to heal these past lives I felt much anger and mistrust of people and the masculine energies in particular.

For a year after the initiation my integration was marred by a self mis-perception which was rebalanced by *Kamaq Wageaq,* when we next met. According to my vision I was innocent except for the incident when I was at school. I began to make peace with the persecution and its effects on my psyche, but I also felt a disconnection from people. My inability to relate to them saddened me. Kamaq Wageaq asked me about this and told me it was based on my visions during initiation. He said that the reason I had seen this one incident only of my own cruelty was because he had cleared my Karmic slate prior to this. He had missed that one incident and so it remained. The effect of this caused me to separate from my humanness rather than making peace with it. He told me to close my eyes and again visions swamped me – I saw myself as the defender of the weak and victimized, taking lives, enacting violence in order to bring justice, not waiting for God, but rather taking the law into my own hands. Seeing this was such a relief – I was human after all and I was still a warrior.

I understood why it was important for me to surrender to the Will of the Creator. In past lives I had flouted and ignored universal law in favor of speedy justice and had paid dearly for it, with my life – many times. But more importantly I paid with my faith and trust. The integration of this initiation brought duality - light and heavy vibration, the masculine and feminine, humanness and spirituality, life and death. Many times over the following two years I remembered *Hatun Runas'* words, when I had dropped the *Chakana*. The black and white *Chakana* symbolizes the balance of the male and female energies, the sun and moon, the dualities. It was handed to me and I dropped it! I had no choice but to re-own that balance within myself the hard way, and the only way I knew, by going through it. And so I did.

The Andean tradition does not refer to light and dark, as is taught by many religious and wisdom schools. We relate to energy by its frequency type – light vibrations and heavy vibrations. I appreciate the value of this, because judgment is removed from ones perception. Instead of viewing things, people, circumstances as good or bad I now look at the degree of balance or imbalance they hold of light and heavy energy. It's possible now to view people without fearing them and with compassionate understanding of why circumstances or people are as they are. Without fear there is no judgment. Our conditioning teaches us when we perceive things as bad, to shy away or become fearful. There are those attracted to 'the bad things' for the sake of rebellion. We are drawn to heavier frequencies, 'the bad things' when we work to understand our shadow. We are human, and as such carry this duality. Significant to our evolution is recognizing and accepting our shadow. When we view consciously without judgment or fear a situation or person, understanding the underlying dynamic, our perspective changes and our tolerance increases.

The Andean Tradition teaches that humans are made up of light energies *Sami,* and heavy energies *Hucha.* This polarity or graduation is essential to the human state. When these energies are imbalanced, it results in discomfort. For example, a person who carries too much *Sami* will be ungrounded, disconnected from the Earth, flighty, inconsistent, and un-focused and have difficulty concentrating and functioning well in physical reality. A person carrying too much *Hucha* will express the shadow of their human state as anger, sullenness, depression, aggression and selfishness, being subjective and reactive.

From the Shamanic view the shadow is an energetic reflection of ourselves; it is the 'other self', which in most people is un-owned. The shadow is the opposite of our light, the part of us which is capable of absolutely anything, good or bad and while it remains un-owned it is dangerous to us, our environment and others. An un-owned shadow will result in unconscious, reactive behavior; the more severe the circumstances, the more extreme the behavior of the shadow. For example a person living in a war may be capable of murder and rape and yet in more normal circumstances would abhor such actions.

While dreaming, a student and fellow initiate experienced her shadow in its true energetic state – literally an external shadow, directly in front of and facing her. When the shadow presents itself so clearly it needs conscious acknowledgement and ownership. I experienced my shadow as splintered facets of myself when I came face to face with it. At this point it must be lovingly embraced into self. While it is separate it is a renegade, ungoverned by consciousness and at its most dangerous. Once our shadow is owned, others actions and reactions become clear and our responses to their shadow become calmer. This process is imperative in the journey of human spiritual development.

Each of the four elements, earth, air, fire and water, expresses duality. The elements are governed by universal law and cannot act independently outside of these laws, as humans can; the elements are manifested within the dimension of duality and are expressed through duality. If any element is stagnant or blocked within us, it creates havoc. We then experience the dense, heavy vibration of that element, for example the shadow or *Hucha* of fire can be rage, hatred, jealousy; the shadow of water can be melancholy or sadness; of air limiting obsessive thought, and of earth it can be insecurity and materialism.

The elements frequencies vary also. Earth has a much denser, heavier vibration to Air, which is light and airy. Neither is better, they are simply different, and equally essential to the makeup and balance of life. Within nature the density of vibration is expressed in all manifestations, equally acknowledged and honored as part of the greater whole. At an atomic level the molecules and atoms of a leaf have a denser vibration than the spaces in between those atoms; however both the atoms and the spaces are necessary for manifested life in physical reality.

YANANTIN AND MASANTIN

Duality has a further manifestation, the masculine and feminine, known in the Andean Tradition as *Yanantin* and *Masantin*. *Yin* and *Yang* in the Eastern Teachings, contain within them each a small portion of the other. Nothing is absolute in this world. For example the Earth is feminine, but the Apus or mountain spirits, the higher individualized expressions of the Earth, can be masculine or feminine. However in the Andean tradition we also perceive that everything in this world is birthed through the feminine, including the masculine. Everything is first feminine and then the masculine develops.

The balance of these two energies is essential for harmony. They are equal but different, each naturally fulfilling certain expressions, specific to its makeup. The Sun, *Inti* and the moon, *Mama Kia* are good examples. Each essential in our Solar system to maintain life on planet Earth and each with its own natural function, making possible the ongoing function of the other. They are interdependent, as they function separately, and together they create the environment in which life manifests and perpetuates itself.

Separateness and interdependence exists throughout nature and in humans. We contain both *Yanantin* and *Masantin*, and it is important that we own and balance them within us, ensuring our expressions, actions and manifestations are balanced. With balance comes harmony of both Yanantin and Masantin, together side by side, contained within the same space; much like the sun and moon co existing in the skies.

Sadly our societies lack this balance, expressing separation of the masculine and feminine. In our economic, political, social, environmental and religious structures the masculine has dominated and the feminine disempowered. Our physical reality is a reflection of our internal make up; a balanced mind will think and create in a balanced way but an imbalanced mind will think and create its imbalances. So it is within our societies; we have created imbalanced structures within our western societies; imbalance reflective of us and perpetuated by social conditioning.

To correct this imbalance many women operate through the expression of the masculine energy in their roles, and the men the expression of the feminine. Women, in their desire to 'prove' their equality to men operate more and more through their strength, determination, logic and action based selves; sometimes to the point of abandoning their gentler, creative, intuitive, receptive natures. They find themselves continually rescuing, fixing and doing. After years of this behavior they come to resent their roles finding no pleasure there. At the same time men feel disempowered as they move more into passive supportive roles; attempting to become more 'feeling' based until they too become resentful of their roles, having abandoned their strength.

Unfortunately this is a new expression of the imbalance between the masculine and feminine and is not the healing of these two energies. All humans deserve the right to live through balanced expression of both their masculine and feminine selves, through strength and vulnerability, logic and feeling, receptivity and externalization, through doing and being. We have the right and deserve to be whole. The imbalance of masculine and feminine energy has nothing to do with sexual orientation, or the choices of sexual expression that exist for us.

In my work I counsel couples whose relationships are in trouble. So often the problem comes back to the imbalances of Yanantin and Masantin in the individuals, which in turn affect the relationship.

A woman operating in her masculine energies, in need of deeper connection to the feminine, will be attracted to a man she perceives as gentle, nurturing, the very qualities she needs to own in herself. The man needing to own his masculine self in a more healed way is drawn to her for her strength and independence. Unfortunately the attraction becomes repellant with time, as disillusionment sets in. She finds him weak and he finds her domineering. Looking outside ourselves for what we need to own internally, creates havoc in relationships. Its expressions are vast; strong men attracted to softer women, only to find them weak and dependent, woman seeking strength in their men only to find them dominant and controlling. The variables in these role plays and attractions are infinite and often subtle.

The solution in relationship is simple – the purpose of relationship is not to fulfill us. The fulfillment of self must come from within; we must look to ourselves for the fulfillment of our needs and not to others. If, for example, a person in a relationship feels they need more attention from their partner, and don't receive it, they feel resentful and upset; they need to take responsibility for their needs first. Expecting others to fulfill us is usually a disappointing experience. By fulfilling our own need first we are able to approach our partner from a desire to share rather than a place of need. The purpose of relationship like everything in our lives; our work, family, friends, etc, is a platform to express who we are, an opportunity for us to show through our actions, words and choices who we are to those around us, and to better understand that expression for ourselves, as it is mirrored back at us through the eyes of another.

We cannot correct the imbalance between the masculine and feminine by changing our roles in society: women becoming providers while men become nurturers, as people are best suited to what comes naturally to them, not gender based, but based on talent and natural affinity. The correction lies in the individual, in finding that natural balance of these two energies and being able to express them fearlessly, to draw on both our male and female energies as need or circumstance arise, enabling us the most truthful expression of ourselves in our lives.

For example, parenting is considered to be made up of a male and female role, with mothers seen traditionally as the nurturers and fathers as the disciplinarian but within the individual parent, irrespective of gender, exists the ability to nurture and reinforce boundaries, in varying degrees, depending on the individual. If the individual is balanced with truthful expression of these two qualities, the Yanantin and Masantin, wholeness is formed.

It is individuals, as a part of the collective consciousness, who create the structures on our planet; business, social and family structure. If the individual is operating from balance, the collective consciousness has a greater chance of becoming balanced and the structures created will be balanced. While there is dissention between the sexes, there is internal disharmony between the *Yanantin* and *Masantin*. Healing requires a healthy dose of self-knowledge, recognizing and understanding the male and female aspects of ourselves, our expressions of them, unconditional self-acceptance, and the understanding that these two equally powerful aspects are interdependent.

In nature balanced Yanantin and Masantin create harmony; the Sun and Moon in the sky, Water and Air, Fire and Earth, so different from each other but co existing to support and balance each other. If we as individuals own this balance within ourselves, then as a society we will create harmony. It is the key to the next cycle of continued life on our planet.

Yanantin and *Masantin* also represent the energy of light and dark perceived through religious conditioning as being 'bad' and 'good'. The Andean Tradition offers a different perception. Darkness or Blackness is the color of night and relates to the receptive feminine. Black absorbs all colors, power and knowledge. Gestation occurs in darkness, whether in a seed planted in the Earth or whether a foetus developing in the womb. Darkness represents potential growth, manifestation and life, which when birthed brings new life in a physically manifested form. White light relates to the masculine, giving force, and makes possible individual colours, as in rainbows or prisms. White light represents the manifested state as the darkness represents the void.

CHAPTER THIRTEEN

INTENTION, PRINCIPLES & THE CHAKANA

In 2003, I was again invited to Peru for initiation, and went as a different person. This was my 3.3 initiation, the *Suyu Llagta Alto Misayoq* level. I felt I had been restructured at a very deep level and in truth probably had been. I felt stronger and clearer, with significant changes in my perceptions of others. In the past I found it hard to be myself totally with others. This was born out of mistrust of people; I loved them, served them but did not feel safe exposing my inner self to others. This left me defensive. The clarity I now experienced made me aware of the 'humanness' in others, but also the understanding of its origins and make up. My new relationship with my own 'humanness', all those bits of me that I would have preferred didn't exist made it easier to look at others, their faults and accept them as they are. I understood that what I saw was their wounding and it did not alter their essence, their soul.

POWER TO MANIFEST

There were a number of us traveling to Peru, leaving South Africa in two groups, within a few days of each other. We had major strikes at the time in the airline and airport staff. The airline we were to travel with had not had a plane leave the ground in more than a week. Two days before our flight I queried it with the travel agent as I felt a slight twinge of panic. She assured me the negotiations for wage increases were almost complete and everyone would be back at work shortly. The day before our departure there was still no resolution. I decided to take action. That night I performed ceremony to ask Ille Tecsi Wiracocha to help us. The response felt positive and during the ceremony I saw Kamaq Wageaq's face clearly and I knew somehow we would leave the next day.

The next morning the strike was still in progress and the airport was in chaos. There were passengers who had been in South Africa for more than a week in transit (at the airport) waiting to go to South America. The travel agent came to the airport to assist and when it became apparent a flight would in fact leave, she called our (second) group, due to leave a few days later, and told them to come to the airport now. They made it, some without having bought their foreign exchange, some without all their luggage, but they came.

Three hours after our flight was due to leave the plane took off, with a crew the airline had pulled out of retirement (literally), some of whom were physically accosted by the strikers while trying to reach the airport. We held our breath collectively, aware something could go wrong at any moment to change our plans. Every person on that flight cheered and clapped when we left the runway. The strike continued for days after our departure and ours was the only South African Airways flight to take off, either domestically or internationally, during the weeks that the strike raged.

Such is the power of intention, the connection and support of nature and Spirit in our daily lives. Some think spiritual power impractical, but in truth Spirit created the physical and is totally adept at managing its creation.

In the Andean tradition, the masters teach use of the senses in a specific sequence to manage energy and to manifest realities. The qualities are as follows:

Imagination

Visualization

Concentration

Sensation

Intention*

*Intention is the driving force, empowering the other four stages. Science has proven matter is transformed when exposed to focused 'mind', a term better described as consciousness, and directing this powerful awareness, our consciousness, through our will, is our intention. Intention, for better or worse has driven the destiny of the human race, into wars, materialism; it moves organizations, religions and societies; creates technical advancement, great artworks and drives human beings to seek the truth.

The Andean tradition offers a special perception of time and space, and this perception plays a vital role in the process of directing intention. The past, present and future is not perceived in a linear fashion but rather we perceive an eternal present. What happened to us yesterday affects us still, we feel it, we carry the memory of it and its energy manifestations are still present in our body. As such because we perceive the past is still with us, it is present. The future, in turn, is a virtual reality, a possibility that exists but has not yet happened, therefore it too is present.

This does not mean we are stuck with the impact of all our past experiences, because through the conscious use of the elements, with a pure intention, we transform the energetic effects of the past, and the future, in the present time from negative or hurtful into positive and empowering intention.

Another interesting perception in the Andean Tradition is the past perceived in front of us and the future behind us. We have lived the past, we know it therefore it is in front of us, clearly seen and the future as yet unlived is behind us. This is contrary to western perception, which perceives the future ahead. The Inkas found the Spanish conquistadors odd for this reason, and described them as having eyes in the back of their heads looking to the future, which to them was totally illogical.

Consciously using our intention we take responsibility for our reality, as everything is our manifestation, whether deliberately or through the law of attraction, which states what is held within us; thoughts, emotions, beliefs, patterns, will be reflected back at us through the external world. Any sense of victimization is removed and replaced with empowerment, enabling us to change things.

THE THREE PRINCIPLES

In Peru's sacred valley, my fellow travelers and I assisted on the third Level initiation, partaking in our own initiation several days later. This initiation was gentle and special for me. I always felt in the spiritual journey we must transcend the archetypes, the roles we take on and portray in our lives i.e.: the warrior, the teacher, the healer, the rescuer etc. This initiation proved me correct. Put simply, it is a journey beyond what is formalized and known into an energetic realm of un-manifested possibility and forms of being. This initiation brought an upward and outward movement of consciousness into the *Hanaq Pacha,* and a purification of the Divine fire within.

After the difficult integration I experienced with the previous initiation I was grateful for the gentle subtlety of this one. It was however, no less powerful. I started feeling I was finally, consistently owning and becoming a living expression of the fifth element – love. I felt expansion in my heart, the beautiful warmth of joyfulness independent of external factors or people, and was entirely my own expression. When feeling sick, or suffering in my human state, this heart expression remained intact and strong. Imagine feeling ill and happy at the same time? This is what I observed in the masters on the first workshop I attended. The principle of *Munay* was birthed right inside me.

The Andean tradition teaches three principles, the first being *Yachay. Yachay* means knowledge in its basic expression, its higher expression is wisdom. It is knowledge, which is integrated through experience and externalized as wisdom. Our pursuit of knowledge must be driven by this intention. Knowledge is accessed by conventional methods of reading books etc. and through working with the elements. For example; a rock, billions of years old, has witnessed much. When we recognize the consciousness of that rock and realize it is no different in essence to our own consciousness, only the vibration frequency varies, we can communicate with it at a conscious level. The well of wisdom, of knowledge within that rock is infinite and we are able to tap into it.

Yanchay is accumulated knowledge put into practice. We must live what we know, mastering it in daily living. There are many gifts from this practice; simply it enables self-improvement and our best expression in the world.

The second principal, *Llankay,* relates to work, labor and productivity. It is an honest living and being honest in your work; working for the betterment and greater good of yourself, family, community and humanity the greater family. The nature of the labor is unimportant – a humble profession or an acclaimed one. What is relevant is honest performance and love for the doing, and the work. For most humans work or productivity may have greater goals, but the bulk is experienced as daily routine. It is easy in this daily routine to lose passion, inspiration and drive for what we do but when love is the motivation, it keeps us present in our work and makes joy a part of the daily struggle. In Western society, work is a means to an end – money. But in the Andean Tradition money or the means to live, although important and necessary, is a by-product of the opportunity to do a good job, with passion, creativity and effort as an expression of who we are.

A lack of productivity is theft, not contributing to the growth and expansion of our communities, but expecting others to provide and maintain them without our efforts.

Munay is the third principle – This word simply means love and is the principle present in all others. It is not the love between a man and a woman, a mother and a child, although these interactions can contain the infinite expressions of *Munay*. It is the expression of unconditional love. It contains a deep-seated compassion for all livings things and their suffering. It is the connection to and joy of the beauty of nature, the song in your heart when you see a magnificent sun set, bathing the sky in violet, red and orange, or the sound of the oceans rhythmic tranquility as it caress your mind.

The great Masters, who walked this planet in ages past, lived, expressed and embodied *Munay* - unconditional love for all of creation. It begins with falling in love with oneself, then that gentle powerful frequency expands to envelope our brothers and sisters, all creatures in creation and the Great Creator of the universe – *Ille Tecsi Wiracocha*. To flow in love with all creation is the ultimate experience of bliss.

THE CHAKANA

"I stood under the Cosmic Chakana in Sacsayhuaman, which Kamaq Wageaq said, "Is a gateway, a portal to the Cosmos". To me it was beautiful. It displays the upper half of the Chakana with seven steps instead of the usual three. As I stood there, I felt I was being transported through time. My eyes were closed and my arms started to move of their own volition, slowly and gently but with certainty. I let go of my thoughts about what I was doing, letting this feeling unfold. My arms stretched out at my sides, steadily moving upwards. As they passed each step of the Chakana, I felt my hands 'scoop' the energies of that step. Once my hands rose above my head, they drew down powerfully, my arms bending and the energy collected in my hands and entered my body through my crown.

This was a strange experience for me because I am a shy person, and to do something like this, especially in front of others was unusual. I can only say these were the actions of my essence and not my human self." - Silvina, Sacsayhuaman, Cuzco

The simple, powerful principles of *Munay*, *Llankay* and *Yanchay* are contained within the teachings of the *Chakana*. The *Chakana* is the ancient cross of the Inkas. In many Peruvian sites, carvings, engravings and statues of the *Chakana* are to be found: at the ruins of Macchu Picchu, Pisac, Ollyantaitambo, Sacsayhuaman in Cuzco, but the oldest representation of the *Chakana* is in the valley of Caral on the central Peruvian coast and is said to date back 16000 years; it is eroded but still intact. When reconstructing, another *Chakana* in Bolivia at the archaeological site of Tiawanaku was uncovered. Here a *Chakana* pool was built atop the seven stepped Sun Temple. This *Chakana* would have been filled with sacred waters, reflecting the stars at night. It is believed it was used to 'read the heavens'. The word *Chakana* is derived from the Quechua language from the words '*Chaka*, meaning 'bridge' and '*Chakachay*' meaning 'to build a bridge'.

The *Chakana* embodies the symbols, principles, truths and entire cosmology of the Andean Tradition. It is the embodiment of all existing knowledge and wisdom. It is the Andean priest's Mandala, containing the seven directions (north, south, east, west, interior, below and above), the five elements earth, air, fire, water and 'Munay' – unconditional love – the fifth element, all their qualities and the principals of this ancient tradition.

It shows the origins of the human race and the path of healing and balancing ourselves as individuals. It represents everything in time and space and everything in timeless space. Created through sacred geometry, it contains geometrical shapes. It is a symbol of infinite depth and simplicity.

It is a cosmic ordering device, a giant cosmic ideogram because it represents so many things. For example, there are *Chakanas* for agriculture, representing the solstices and equinoxes, and the changing seasons. The agricultural Chakana also contains the Solar, Venusians and Lunar calendars – three separate calendars with different qualities working together in synchronicity to aid agriculture.

When the *Chakana* is on a flat surface, the underneath signifies one thing, and the top another. To better understand this, think of the human hand, we are unable to hold things with the exterior of our hands but with the palm side we can grasp and hold things. We think of it simply as a hand but there is duality within it and its functions. The *Chakan*a is the same. One side is active, applied for certain effects, the other passive applied for different effects. The one side is chaos, the other order; one side is the void and the other manifestation. This is why we refer to it as a cosmic ordering device.

On each step, either side of the *Chakana* there are a number of symbols. These symbols express meaning, energy characteristics and concepts. These symbols include the three worlds, the animal and plant kingdoms, the moon and the sun, the feminine and the masculine, our ancestors, the spiritual hierarchy, our community, our species, our creator and many other aspects of creation.

Looking at the *Chakana,* the top arm faces east and reflects the fire element, the bottom arm faces west representing the earth element,and the right arm faces south and reflects water, while the left arm is in the north reflecting the air element. Wearing the *Chakana,* the southern arm sits over our feminine side, the left side of our bodies and the northern arm sits over our masculine right side of our bodies. The Andeans believe a human being must walk facing the east. Not literally, but symbolically. We walk with our hearts and consciousness directed to where the sun - light rises, keeping our shadow behind us.

The *Chakana* also represents the three worlds, the bottom section – *Uju Pacha*, middle section – Kay Pacha and upper section – Hanaq Pacha, and the animal guardians of these worlds, snake, puma and condor respectively.

The *Chakana* contains four sections in between the arms each with three steps, a total of twelve steps. These twelve steps at first glance represent the twelve months of the year, or the twelve Luna cycles, perceived by the Incas as making a greater cycle, a year. However, these steps have a deeper significance; they contain the principles of living. The three steps on the bottom left side of the *Chakana* relate to the *Munay, Llankay and Yakay*. *Munay* as love of self, love of humanity and love of *Ille Tecsi Wiracocha*. *Llankay* as labouring with love for the betterment of our community and for humanity. *Yakay* as wisdom, knowledge as applied experience becoming wisdom.

Below the *Chakana* shows the directions, the elements, their qualities, the balance of the male and female, the void and other symbols.

The Symbolism of the Chakana

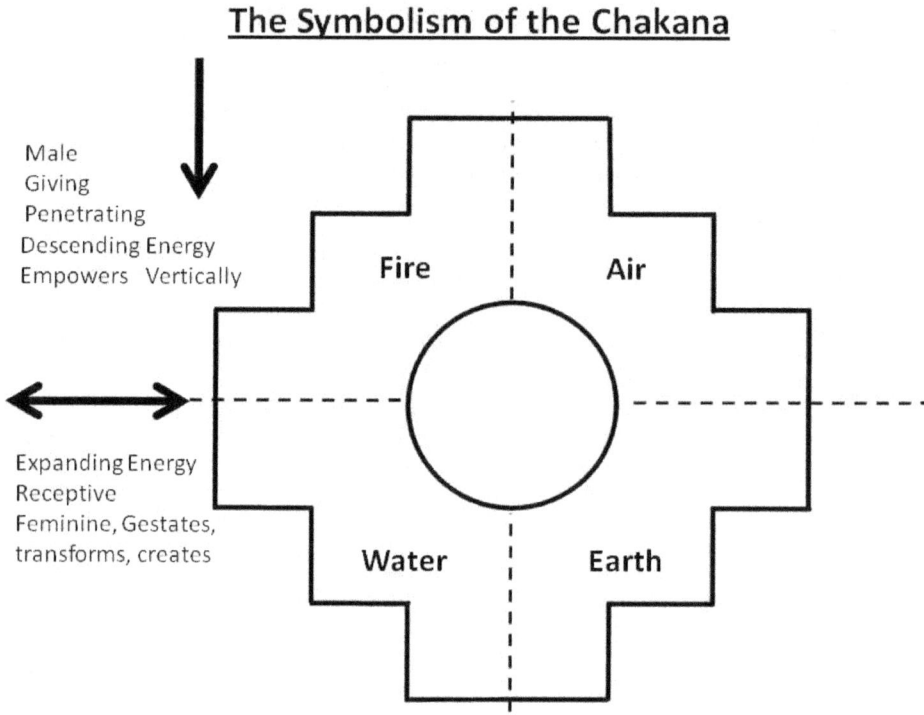

Male
Giving
Penetrating
Descending Energy
Empowers Vertically

Expanding Energy
Receptive
Feminine, Gestates,
transforms, creates

The Symbolism of the Chakana

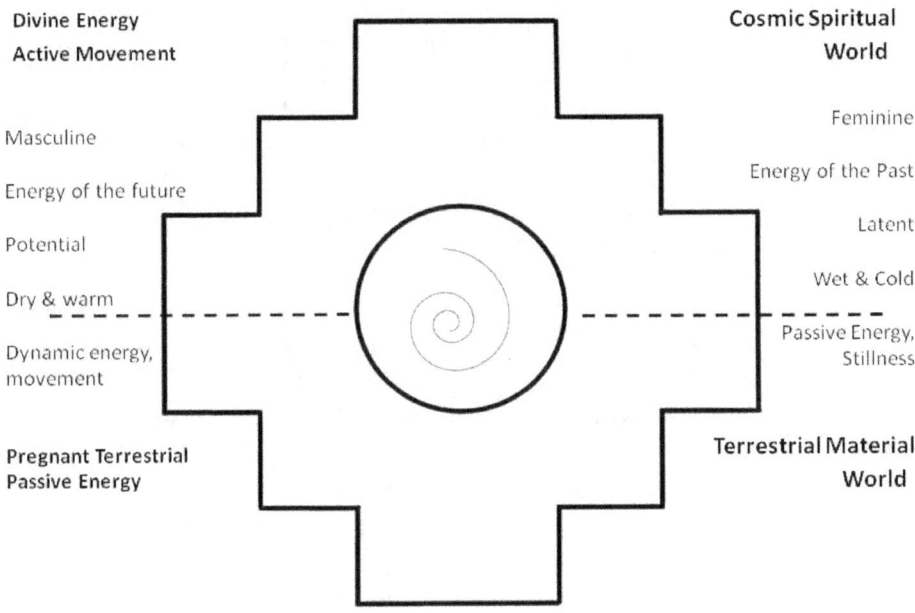

External Face of the Chakana

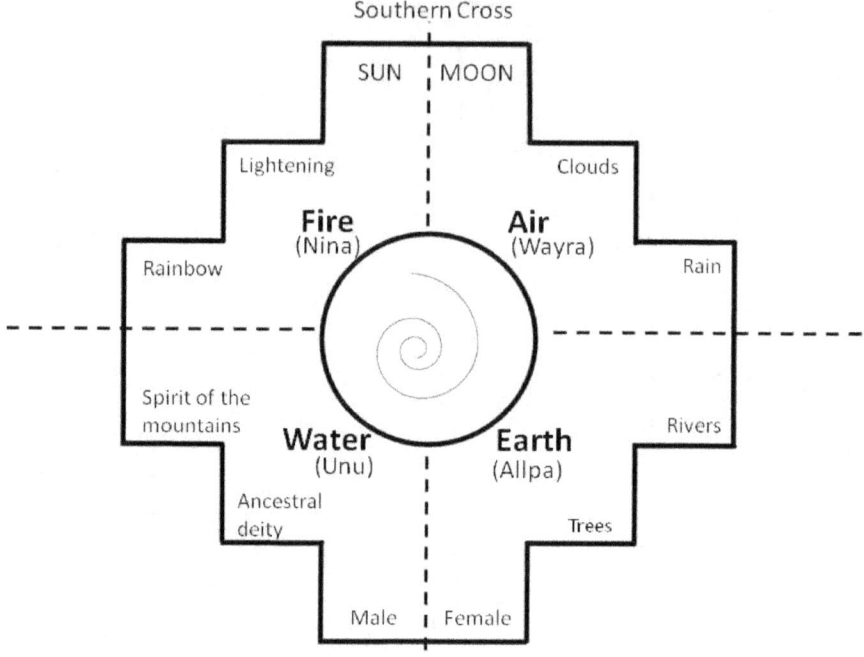

Internal Face of the Chakana

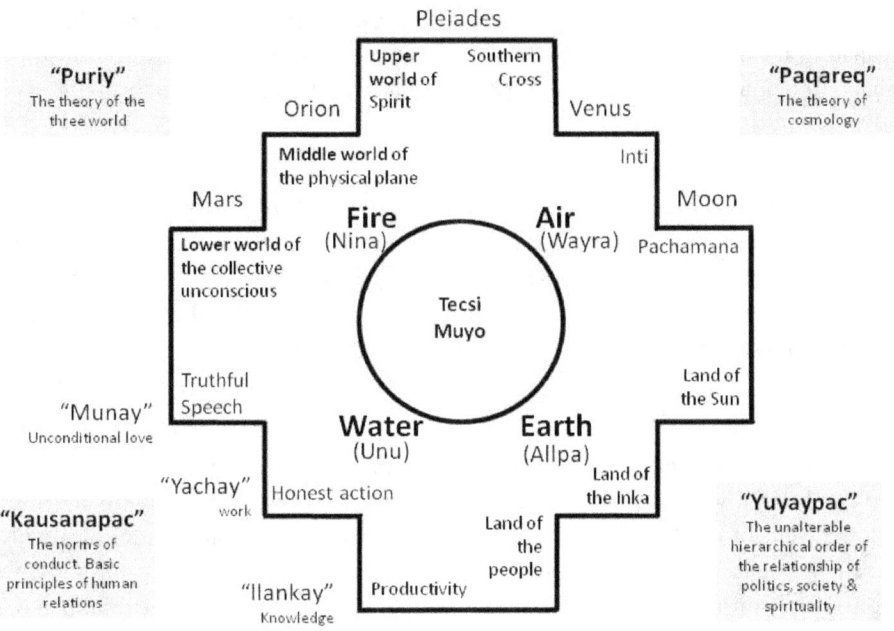

In the physical realm – the world we live in, nothing is absolute. Within everything in our physical world, the realm of duality, an aspect of its opposite is contained. As mentioned previously, the masculine contains a small percentage of the feminine and within the feminine is a small percentage of the masculine. In the diagram of the *Chakana* in the centre is the void. The void is the origin, beyond creation, and it is in there that the absolute exists. The centre of the *Chakana* also depicts the fifth element, emanating from the void. This element expressed is love. Love cannot be measured nor gauged, it belongs beyond time and space, beyond creation and it belongs to the void.

The four elements move towards the centre of the *Chakana* and the fifth element expands outwards. Love is balance, equilibrium and harmony. Love is our original nature and when our minds, bodies and emotions flow in balance we experience our nature, love. It is unconditional love for all including self, where we arrive when choosing to live our lives as authentic human beings.

The *Chakana* expresses the activation of the fifth element and its application. We must love and be in love with ourselves, not in a sexual, vain, emotional or selfish sense, but with the truth of our being, our essence. This love applies in our relationship with *Ille Tecsi Wiracocha*, loving and serving our Creator and all in existence with body, mind, emotion and spirit. Through serving our Creator we serve also our fellow human beings in love. The way we live raises the sub conscious energies of our planet, which affects our human brothers and sisters, assisting their evolution so all of humanity can experience their internal nature and return to the Creator.

The *Chakana* superimposed over a human body, shows the masculine energy on the right hand side. The feminine energy is on the left. Three of our *chakras* are in the upper section of the Chakana; the throat, third eye and crown chakras, and three in the lower section, the solar plexus, naval and root *chakras*. The centre of the *Chakana* corresponds with the heart centre, the centre of our energy system. Through the heart centre we access the experience of Divine truth, our soul. And through our heart centre we experience the void, the absolute. It is safe to say the centre of our body exists in the void and the access point is our heart centre.

Through the levels of initiation we learn to be energy masters, understanding how to manage energy in the void, timeless space and the non physical dimensions and in manifested reality, time space reality and earth. We learn how energies from our physical reality are transmuted through the void and redirected in their transmuted state back into our physical reality. This is done in accordance with the natural laws. Going against natural law is to go against creation, The Creator and our natural evolution. In the Andean Tradition this is the definition of 'evil'.

Managing energy this way is the definition of mastery and the true expression of power. This power cannot be seen, which is true of all real expressions of power, but can be felt and experienced. External power in the form of possessions and dominance is purely window dressing, and pursuing this type of power brings neither substantial happiness nor fulfilment.

The balance of the masculine and feminine and the elements within us, create a state of wholeness, which reflects in our energy field. When our energy field is undisturbed, we experience a state of being described as 'protection' in a natural way; we are not affected by others negative thoughts or feelings. External circumstances and situations have no effect when balance is retained. The *Chakana* symbolises that state of balance and generates the energy of it. This is shown through the following experience described by a member of the Andean Community in South Africa.

"One morning driving to work in peak hour congested traffic, I felt the stress levels rising in me. Next moment a car tore out of a side road, perpendicular to the road I was on, at high speed. The driver ignored the stop street and barely missed hitting the stop sign. I reacted quickly, swerving safely out of my lane, avoiding collision.

I was beside myself with shock. I started shaking, feeling my blood sugar dropping instantly. At that moment I felt the Chakana I was wearing around my neck 'heat up'. It became so warm that for a few moments it was uncomfortable against my chest. I could feel the shape very distinctly against my skin. The warmth started to spread across my chest and then a sense of calm came over me. By the time I arrived at work I was totally calm and myself again." - Claudelle

The Andean priest uses the *Chakana* to reinstate balance, emotionally, mentally and energetically, and on a cellular level.

The *Chakana* is a regulator of energies.

CHAPTER FOURTEEN

KURAQ AKULLAQ – MASTER OF THE COCA

I accessed, for the first time in my life, a great peace with the masculine energies, and especially in men. I was no longer challenged by it and no longer felt lessened by it. Rather I felt safe in the gentleness of the masculine and took pleasure in the security I found there. This was a relief after lifetimes of challenge and suffering in my interaction with this energy. I had come full circle. My healing in this was complete.

There was magnificent flow in the energy of abundance – a deep knowing born out of absolute trust in relation to my human needs and support including money, people, the elements and life. Visualization, mental imagery and affirmation cannot create that feeling. It is born within a person living in trust of themselves and their lives. Arriving here is a journey, and life becomes the manifestation.

My sensitivity was growing too. I did not understand the purpose of my perceptions through this sensitivity – it showed me a pattern I held so deeply I had accepted it as a part of my nature. My next initiation would present this to me very clearly.

This sensitivity came in gradual stages of perception. I would think of a person, no one in particular, and became aware of their thoughts and mental patterns. A few weeks later I began feeling their feelings – it was no longer mental, it had become emotional. Then a while later I realised I was mirroring people's emotional and mental energies back at them, spontaneously. I felt their energy, their thoughts and feelings and would engage it and present it to them in turn. It took time but finally, I was able to sustain the emotional and mental awareness without engaging the energies personally but it took effort, and an open heart was imperative.

During this time I realized the various forms of energetic protection I used were no longer working. No matter what I tried I felt other peoples 'stuff'. I focused on keeping myself earthed and maintaining connection to light constantly. I also felt the effectiveness of maintaining open and flowing energy centres. I realised protection was no longer necessary, rather than concern of the impact of external energies I began impacting the environment with my energy. For example, if I entered a room full of people, I would usually use my protection to keep their energies at a safe distance. Now I simply expanded my own energy and brought that into the room. It was simple and worked like a charm.

In this state of mind, I again prepared to journey to Peru for my fourth level of initiation – the *Kuraq Akulleq* level – the most profound so far, bringing access of the sixth element.

I was honoured to undertake this initiation, as one of the first within our community and also as a bringer of this consciousness to Africa within my tradition.

We met with our Master, *Kamaq Wageag in Lima*. Our group of ten all originated from the South African community. We flew to Piura in the north of Peru beginning our twenty day journey. Our initiation spanned the length and breadth of the area that had encompassed the *Inkan Empire*. In each area we were exposed to the cultures that made up the Empire, meeting Shamans, masters and modern mystics, exposed to their work through ceremony, participating in their rituals or their teachings.

Our journey took us through all types of terrain - coast, desert, mountains, valleys, jungle with sweltering humidity, altitudes of great height and freezing temperatures. The beauty we witnessed was indescribable - the foliage, flowers, insects, animals, places and people were absorbed in a whirlwind of sensory stimulation. This trip would have exhausted the average traveller but this was initiation. We experienced it all with heightened awareness to the life around and within us, extraordinary levels of vitality, our bodies feeling hunger only when food was available, tired only when a bed was before us.

SAN PEDRO & AYAHUASCA

On the first day of initiation and almost immediately upon arrival in Piura we left for *Huancabamba*, a journey of about six hours. The terrain reminded me of parts of South Africa – semi-arid, dessert similar to the Karoo. By mule we made our way through rocky mountain paths, with the Andes rising up on the right, into a valley with a spectacular lake, to meet with our first master - a shaman of the *Huaringas* lakes called Simon - our first ceremony began.

This was a ceremony of the power plant *San Pedro*. We formed a circle on the edge of the lake around an altar Simon erected, the perimeter of which was *Chonta* wood and metal swords. There followed a reading in Spanish of sacred verses, including biblical reference of the Virgin Mother and spitting different aromatic perfumes; rose, Patchouli and *Aqua de Florida,* alcohol based flower water in blessing of the sacred verses and the directions.

We underwent a cleansing ceremony in the freezing lake waters, clear sweet water directly from the mountains. We waded in, dunked ourselves, and drank seven sips of the water. We had to air dry. Simon stood off at a distance and in turns we went to stand before him. He ran the flat side of a sword blade through my energy field and had me face the four directions, kicking away any dense negative energy.

We formed a circle in front of the altar and were handed a flat shell, much like a muscle shell filled with liquid black tobacco and herbs. This liquid is sniffed up the nostrils - left nostril first. This process is called *Zingar* and clears the channels and prepares the spirit for the San Pedro. It's a total shock to the nasal passages and tastes very bitter. We each then read from the book of Sacred Verses. I was asked to open the book at random and choose a verse. It was a verse by the Virgin Mother on serving humanity and the virtue of helping others. This ended the ceremony of cleansing. Simon's personal form of faith was clear – he was both shaman and catholic, referring many times to God and the Virgin Mother and making the sign of the cross.

We hiked back and remounted our mules. My mule's name was Pedro, a very irritating animal indeed. He had one speed and it was slow. On the journey down I had done everything to get his co-operation in riding with the group but Pedro would have none of it. On the ride back I eventually surrendered, accepting everything happens in its time, including Pedro. Once I adopted this attitude my pleasure in my journey was complete. It rained gently, enough to get wet. I enjoyed every moment, feeling the sheer environmental beauty with my face turned up to the sky, receiving the blessings of *Unu Mama*. When I dismounted I was at peace. Pedro was a good teacher, and his teaching – patience, a reminder to take my time with everything.

Wet and covered in mud, we returned to Simon's house in a village near the lake. The area we occupied at Simon's home didn't help. The courtyard was a sea of mud and the only loo, located between the house and a field was simply four walls around a slab of concrete, a rectangular hole in the centre over a hole in the ground. It swarmed with mosquitoes. I smiled thinking in the daylight my rump would look as though it had Chickenpox from mozzie bites - and it did.

While Simon set up for ceremony, we were led to a large empty room with mattresses around the perimeter to meditate and rest.

I entered a meditative state quickly and a window of vision opened up before me. I moved quickly upriver from an aerial perspective. I never saw the water but thick bush on either side of my peripheral vision speeding past. A large dove came into view with something square in its beak, from a distance a postage stamp. As it flew overhead it dropped the square object into my lap. Up close it was a large book.

I became aware of a massive eagle with huge eyes made of a silver reflective substance, like mirrors or shiny metal, positioned in front of me. It was so enormous I was a speck of dust at the point of its beak. I felt confused about the book and asked mentally, "What is this?" I heard an answer in my mind, "The book of your life."

I thumbed through it, seeing only a few pages written on, the rest remained blank. I asked, "Why are they blank?" and I received an answer, "Fill them however you choose."

I was immediately back to normal consciousness and dozed off as we were called to present ourselves for the ceremony.

In an area off to one side of the house and open to the elements Simon and his assistant set up chairs for us in a semi-circle, with an altar laid out on the dirt floor. The centre cloth had the same swords of *Chonta* and metal, forming a perimeter. The altar held an array of unusual tools including a variety of perfumed waters, preserved herbs, animal claws, a long thick plait of human hair, a pink and a black brazier, and off to the side a large pot of greenish fluid with star shaped slices of *San Pedro* cactus floating languidly in it. The walls were draped with flags from all over the world symbolising the unity of humanity. And hanging from the ceiling above the altar was a dead dehydrated squirrel.

The ceremony began with the spitting of various scented waters. The fluid is sipped and sprayed from the mouth. I have done this many times with Aqua De Florida and it is not pleasant. It is a little like sipping cologne that leaves one's mouth and lips numb and corrugated. Lively traditional music played while we danced and swayed, laughing.

A young woman with a beautiful healthy baby seated herself and proceed to breast feed her child. This symbolised innocence and love invited into the space for the ceremony. We touched the Earth as Simon called the winds of the various directions and repeatedly he gave thanks to the lake's waters and the rain.

Simon drew my dear friend Limor, into the centre of the circle, cleansing her with a long silver sword as he had done to us at the lake. He handed her the sword and she became the symbol for Arc Angel Gabriel – whose presence he united with for the ceremony. This channelled purification to all those present in the ceremony.

Simon cleansed us with a mixture of starch and water by flicking a small amount over each of us.

One after the other, we were handed a small glass of San Pedro to drink. The San Pedro cactus is sliced and boiled in liquids – primarily water – producing a bitter tasting green liquid. For our first try we received a small amount, about a third of a glass. A feeling of lightness and humour grew stronger within me as the dancing continued.

Simon channelled for each person, bringing them to the centre of the circle, spitting perfume over them and in chanted melodious verses, told us about ourselves. He told me of service to humanity, good work in all parts of the world, the absence of a man in my life, the goodness of my heart and my destiny.

Lastly he channelled for *Kamaq Wageag*, then pulled me into the centre with *Kamaq Wageag* and spat floral water over us. The master left the circle and Simon proceeded to 'cut' open my energy from the chest to below my belly button, then holding the point of the sword against my heart centre he spat another perfumed water over my heart. Kamaq Wageaq explained the next day that the 'cutting' of my energy was to connect to my essence and the spitting of the flower water was to stimulate it, to blossom and flourish. He explained that although Simon had performed this only on me, it was done for the whole group of initiates present.

He handed me a large brass crucifix saying he had held this a long time and was tired and suffering. *Kamaq Wageaq* again explained that this symbolised Simon – a man whose faith is Catholicism - taking the suffering and density of all present, away.

Simon drank several more glasses of San Pedro. At one point he explained he drank for us as we had elected to have only a small amount.

Simon handed me a falcon claw, with part of the leg attached. He held the leg area and I held the actual claw in my right hand. He told me to pull it away from him. Gently I tugged until I had freed it and immediately he gave thanks to the lake. *Kamaq Wageaq* explained this part of the ceremony was for me personally, the falcon claw symbolised the power to take, to capture what I want from the world.

Simon handed me a glass of mixed alcohols, asking me to drink half the glass while he drank the other half. He handed me a small white rose and Simon held another. Together we ate the petals. He said the process was to return my heart to its original purity. I was told this was for me to flourish and help me fulfil my destiny.

Simon brought the ceremony to closure saying we were together as a group from all over the world for the betterment of humanity and that made him very happy. He also told us we would come again.

The second experience with San Pedro was a very different ceremony. I found the power plant itself raised my spirits, giving me vitality but there were no hallucinations or visions. Anything that I did see was really no different than what I experienced normally. In fairness, we only used small doses of the plant and this may have been the reason. However, I felt San Pedro's Spirit to be very gentle by nature.

The second ceremony a few days later, also in the Northern parts of Peru, near the *Tucume* pyramids, was conducted by Orlando a *Morchica* shaman. This culture was ruled by *Sipan* and they were ancestors of the *Incas*. Orlando's ceremonial attire was similar to our vibration. The energy created in the ceremony was also similar to that generated in our own ceremonies – gentle, open hearted, pure and simple.

This ceremony was conducted in an outdoor amphitheatre, with two steps around the perimeter. It was open to the sky and the evening was chilly with cloud cover.

An altar with a row of *Chonta* and metal swords, created a screen behind which Orlando sat. Once we were in place around the perimeter of the circle, Orlando shook our hands and introduced himself.

He blessed his altar using scented waters and his rattle. He did not spit the scented waters but used spritzer bottles instead, a rather unusual method for a shaman.

We were each handed a glass of San Pedro to drink. This was more than double the quantity we had consumed in our first experience. We sat down to meditate with eyes closed.

I felt tired with sleep overtaking me, and struggled to stay awake but eventually relaxed into it. The only vision I had was of two serpents in a vertical position facing one another. They were not touching in any way.

Later we all stood to perform *Zingar*. A large curved shell was used; the point placed under each one's nostril, and tipped slightly as the liquid tobacco was sniffed up the nostrils into the sinus. This process was not easy, or comfortable.

A purification and activation for each individual followed. A large white quartz crystal ball was first placed in front of the third eye, while *Aqua De Florida* was sprayed over the ball and the area. This was repeated at the base of the neck, over each hand, which were held together and cupped. As Orlando did this, he invoked his power to purify each person's mind.

Orlando left the circle to seat himself behind the altar and the row of swords; from there he proceeded to rattle and chant a moving haunting melody for several hours in a slow deep broken voice.

At this point his assistants took over the proceedings. Individually we stood in front of the altar and stamped the earth with our feet. Using two swords called *Gabilanes*, beginning above the head, moving over the throat, neck, arms and legs to the feet, criss-crossing each in constant expert movement, the assistants severed energies, and cleared them.

The same process was repeated using two copper objects called *Cenceros*, similar to cow bells but more elongated and soundless. The *Cenceros* purify the spirit of the physical organs of the body.

We were individually led outside the circle and by shaking and flinging our limbs three times were instructed to kick away density and issues.

The ceremony ended. Orlando said he had kept the dosage low since, not meeting us before, he didn't know our individual state of health and well-being. I had few visions using the San Pedro, but didn't feel it was ineffectual. I understand that if a real connection is made with the spirit of the power plants, a relationship is maintained long after the effects of the ceremony have worn off.

It was my experience on this initiation to access information about my life, my essence and my destiny through the power plant ceremonies and the meetings with the shamans, masters and mystics. Information was given to me by Spirit through nature and connection to power places, and much of what the power plants presented supported what I accessed, especially the *Ayahuasca*.

The experience with this very powerful plant is as alive in my mind as when it happened. It took place in the Amazon jungle with an 84 year old *Ayhuasquero,* the name given to the *Auyuscha* master, with almost sixty years experience working with the plant. Like the San Pedro, the *Auyuscha* is a living plant spirit, accessed and communicated with through the hallucinogenic properties of the plant. I do not recommend you try this at home.

Our ceremony took place in a large circular wooden room with a short enclosed passage that lead to a bathroom, a necessity when taking *Auyuscha* as the plant causes purging – through the bowel and vomiting. Although I had no nausea during the process, others in my group did. On an energetic level one purges all the dense energy within, and I realized during the ceremony, the spirit of the *Auyuscha* feeds on this. The plant kingdom is an extension of the Earth and the Earth energetically takes our dense vibrations and transmutes them into light vibrations.

Thin single mattresses spread along the perimeter of the room created a circular space in the centre, where a burning candle was placed. I was positioned to the right of the *Ayahuaschero*, who sat on a chair with a table to his left. His assistant was present for practical requirements, as the *Ayhuaschero* consumes the power plant with the group, and the effects debilitate the body for the duration - about 5 hours in total. *Kamaq Wageag* did not participate, but was present throughout to assist and empower our processes, something I became grateful for as the evening wore on, as my perception of my physical reality and control over it weakened.

The ceremony began quickly, as the *Ayhuaschero* presented us each with a small glass of brownish green liquid to drink, first blessed with his intentions and cigarette smoke. *Auyuscha* is a vine grown in the Amazon and, with another plant, is prepared into a liquid like the San Pedro.

The concoction took effect in about 30 minutes. I lay on my matt, waiting. I felt a strange sensation take over my body and saw a bright white ball of light travel towards me from above, enter my crown, forcing its way in a grinding, drilling motion into my brain, which burst open with light. This was not a gentle experience, nor was it painful in any way. I ground my teeth as fear caroused through me. What if I lost my mind permanently? I consciously let go and allowed.

The visions began.

The *Ayhuaschero* segmented the experience into sections, Earth (physical), Water (sentimental), Air (mental), Fire (courage and emotions) and finally Spirit. A person is supposed to perceive information about themselves and their evolution during these sessions, information of necessary change or healing in each area of themselves. The Earth session will show patterning or habits related to the physical, material self, the water our sentimental nature, the air our minds and the fire to our emotions and fears. These sections were conducted using a fan of woven leaves. It produced a sound which dominated the session, creating a buzzing perception, causing imagery to become digital – as though made of millions of pixels. I estimated each session took thirty to forty minutes, with breaks of ten or fifteen minutes between. I found this fanning extremely disturbing, and during the breaks my visions were more fluid, with clearer understanding. At times I wished he would stop using the fan.

My vision filled with Mandalas, beautiful intricate Mandalas in soft pastel colours of all hues. *Kamaq Wageag* told us before hand to move towards the light, and it is was my intention from the beginning. I had my energetic sword and in the first session repeatedly cut through the Mandalas in search of the light. At times I would glimpse it but it would vanish, at other times I would see it, move to it and find it was only a reflection. This is so true of physical reality where we cannot truly see or grasp Spirit but glimpse it in nature, in a moment of love or in another human being. In the first two sessions I saw no patterning, only Mandalas, experiencing my powerful desire to reach *Ille Tecsi Wiracocha*.

In the third session I saw three patterns – shown as little signs with the pattern written on them. The patterns I refer to are habits that we all carry physically, emotionally or mentally – habits with no real purpose, to which we lose energy or power. The first pattern wasn't particularly strong and I cut it down with my sword as it arose. The other two related to my relationship with humans. I did not rid myself of them at that time simply because they were not negative – only later on my return to South Africa I realized their potential destructiveness. The first was, my *habit of worrying* about people – all people – friends, family, strangers, clients, everyone. The second was tougher to let go – my *compulsion to help people*, not in their evolution, which is my destiny, but in daily living, in their challenges and their patterns. Later I understood both patterns were a result of lack of trust of my Creator. When we trust the Creator, we must also trust everyone's life processes, knowing their journeys are taking them exactly where they need to be. I questioned how I would express my love and compassion for humanity if I let go of this pattern. Later I would realize the love, unconditional acceptance and wisdom that this initiation brought, coupled with my devotion to humanities evolution, were enough.

The Mandalas continued to flow and fold, manifesting with intricate beauty, but also with a hollow-ness, as though I viewed paintings or drawings as inanimate objects. This disturbed me and I continued to seek out authenticity, constantly looking for light with substance, life, to satisfy my yearning. Twice I glimpsed a face, a being of great light and beauty, ancient and youthful at the same time, a form clothed in simple white robes of living light. 'He' smiled benevolently with infinite kindness and compassion but it was as if I saw 'Him' through muslin – I realize now the veil was thinning.

In between the sessions I received clear information regarding my own life, humanity and the Creator. I was shown how creation formed but was not yet 'breathing', and how *Ille Tecsi Wiracocha* poured 'Himself' into creation giving it life. How, because of this, we must honor and love life in all its forms for it is also to love our Creator. We must care for our human brothers and sisters and all of nature with infinite tenderness, for it is to take care of the living creation. My heart swelled.

Then fear struck me and deep sadness as I thought, "What if the Creator no longer existed outside of Creation? What if Creation had become all there is?" I felt devastation and pushed this thought away, realizing this was my deepest, most hidden fear.

Finally the sessions finished and the disruptive fanning ended. I had arrived in a place of magnificent natural beauty which faded by comparison to the Being standing in the centre of my vision – welcoming me, loving me, and comforting me – all by simply being there. The muslin was gone, the veil lifted and I stood looking upon *Ille Tecsi Wiracocha*. It is impossible to describe in words the feelings, the imagery, the sensations and the love. 'He' led me further into my vision, standing behind a white stone altar on which was placed a book. 'He' spoke - of my destiny, of what is written that cannot be changed, of what I must do and become to fulfill what is written.

The effects of the plant were wearing off and I became aware again of my body, my bowel growling for release, those around me stirring and the images began to fade – I shifted between my vision consciousness and waking reality. It faded altogether. I was left with infinite beauty and peace.

Over several days I processed and assimilated what I had seen and been shown. I looked at my haunting fear squarely; the fear *Ille Tecsi Wiracocha* was absorbed entirely into creation, and creation is all there is, realizing in this dimension of duality our deepest desires, also hosting our deepest fears. The fears are simply not real and exist to give us an appreciation of what is real.

Through the remainder of the initiation this fear would be put to rest without a remnant of doubt, and I would feel the spiritual illumination of 'knowing' fill me – a knowing that cannot be worded nor expressed but only held within.

CHAPTER FIFTEEN

PROPHECIES FOR THE FUTURE

Legend has it that Inti the ancient sun god sent his two children Manco Capac and Mama Ocllo, to help the children of Earth establish better lives. They are said to have emerged out of Lake Titicaca and on an island in the lake, Inti gave them a great golden staff. The staff, called the Tapac-Yauri, was to be used to found the Incan Empire. They would find the location for the centre of the Empire by sticking the staff into the ground. Manco and his sister searched Peru for the right place, but the staff would not penetrate the earth. Finally, they came upon the most beautiful place they had yet seen. They stuck the staff in the ground and it penetrated. This became the city of Cuzco meaning the navel, womb or centre. They conquered the tribes already living there, and incorporated them into the Incan Empire. Manco married his sister and they ruled side-by-side. Thus the Empire began and over time expanded.

Prior to 1438 the *Inca* were, like so many other villages in South America, a small minority. However over the next fifty years they embarked on a conquest that would bring under their control an area that encompassed present-day Peru, Bolivia, northern Argentina, Chile, and Ecuador. Using political systems they established a tribal ruling hierarchy to govern their lands, all regional and local leaders under the rule of the Emperor – the *Inca*.

There are thirteen *Incas* accounted for during the reign of the *Incan Empire*, most with individual titles, some referred to only as the *Inca*. During the rule of the first seven Incas they lived in small villages, found predominantly around their capital city, Cuzco. Inevitably this would change as the Incas were warriors.

Manco Capac founded the *Inca* people and the city of *Cuzco*. He is said to be the incarnation of the Sun-God, *Inti*. The Inca rulers that followed him were *Sinchi Roca, Lloque Yupanqui, Maita Capac, Capac Yupanqui, Inca Roca, Yahuar Huacac, Inca Viracocha, Pachacutec-Inca-Yupanqui, Topa Inca Yupanqui, Huayna Capac, Huascar* Inca and finally *Atahuallpa Inca*.

Expansion of the *Inca Empire* began with *Viracocha's* son *Pachacutec*, a great warrior and seer, and together with his son *Topa* they were the most powerful conquering rulers in South America. During the reign of *Pachacutec* many of the massive masonry structures, for which the *Incas* are famous, were erected, and Cuzco, as the seat of the Empire, became a marvel of hydraulic engineering, agricultural technique, architecture, textile, ceramic and ironwork.

Like the *Mayan* civilisation, the *Incas* left behind them prophesy for the future recorded more than 800 years ago and made by *Inca Pachacutec Yupanqui*. In a civilization of extraordinary warriors and priests of wisdom, Inka Pachacutec was renowned as a healer, healing disease through touch, whose body was illuminated from within, visible by day and night. He was Master and leader of the four *Tawantinsuyos* (four united sections or areas) of the *Incan Empire*.

His given name was *Cusi Yupanqui*. His career began when *Cuzco* came under attack from a rival tribe, the *Chancas*. His father, *Inca Viracocha* the eighth *Sapa Inca* of the Kingdom of Cuzco, abandoned the city, leaving with his heir apparent *Urco*. *Cusi Yupanqui* defended the city, defeating the enemy after which he was proclaimed *Inca*.

He became the ninth *Sapa Inca* of the Kingdom of Cuzco, the fourth of the *Hanan* dynasty, and his wife's name is given as *Mama Anawarkhi*.

In the early part of his reign, he conquered the area from north of modern Lima to Lake Titicaca. It was common practice with the Incas to put their sons in charge of the army, and *Pachacutec* did. By the time he died his son, *Tupac Inca*, had conquered an area which reached in the North all the way to Ecuador. The area conquered in *Pachacutecs* life time consisted of nearly the entire Andes mountain range.

The *Colla* and *Lupaca* people of the Lake Titicaca area were defeated first, and then the *Chanca* to the west, who came close to seizing *Cuzco*, but once defeated offered little resistance. Then *Pachacutec* turned to the North, conquering as far as Quito, Ecuador, including the powerful *Chimú* on the northern coast of Peru. At this point *Topa Inca* took over his father's military role, looking to the South where he conquered all of northern Chile as far as the Maule River, which became the southernmost border of the Empire. His son, *Huayna Capac*, continued to conquer the area which forms the present border between Ecuador and Colombia. At the height of their reign, the *Inca Empire* was the largest nation on earth.

It is believed *Pachacutec* would send messages to the leaders of the lands he wished to conquer, telling them the benefits of joining his empire, and offering them luxurious gifts, such as high quality textiles with a promise that they would be materially richer as subject kings of the Empire. Usually the leaders capitulated.

However, the tribes of the Southern Highlands and the Northern Coast resisted. Violent, brutal battles took place in *Cajamarca*, between the warriors from *Trujillo* and *Cuzco*. The Incas eventually took and retained command of the Highlands and the Northern Coastal area and governed from Cuzco. The *Chimu* of the Northern Coast sided with the Spanish against the *Incas* in the final confrontation when the end of the Empire was at hand. By then the last Inca was dead from Chickenpox, and the Conquistadors success was further assisted by the ensuing power struggle between the last Incas two sons.

Pachacutec reordered his new empire, the *Tahuantinsuyus*, creating a system of government ranging from local leaders to governors of the *suyus,* provinces. *Inca* society was made up of *ayllus*, clans of families living and working together. Each *allyu* was supervised by a *Curaca* or chief. He also established a separate chain of command for the army and the priesthood to ensure that the balance of power was maintained.

The *Sapa Inca* and his wives, *Qoyas* were the supreme rulers of the empire. The *Inca* was usually a political figure however with certain *Incas*, like *Pachacutec*, they also ruled as the High Priest. Within the army the Commander in Chief reported directly to the *Inca* and was supported by the regional army commanders. The High priests ruled over the temple priests, who held similar positions socially to the architects, administrators and army generals. This structure supported *Incan* society for hundreds of years.

The *Incas* built a network of roads, linking the people of the mountains and the lowlands with *Cuzco*. Many of these roads were built at great heights over the mountains, requiring materials to be hauled on foot, at high altitudes. This was, under conditions which could cause illness, if not death today without the assistance of our modern equipment and technology. These roads ensured a system of transport and communication rivaling that of Rome at the time. Today, there remain thousands of miles of road in excellent condition.

Pachacutec rebuilt *Cuzco* into an imperial city and a fitting representation of the Empire. He is also believed to have begun construction of the huge fortress above *Cuzco,* called *Sacsayhuaman*, and credited with the building of *Macchu Picchu.*

The Empire consisted of more than twenty million people. As the empire expanded, incorporating other tribes, the Incas used a universal language – *Quechua*.

The *Incas* were a deeply spiritual people who believed everything was created by the ever-lasting, invisible, and all-powerful *Ille Tecsi Wiracocha*, and they believed in reincarnation.

Inca Pachacutecs son, *Tupac Inca*, peacefully took over reign of the Empire, becoming the next *Inca*, on *Pachacutecs* death. However, in future generations the next *Inca* had to prove their worthiness by winning enough support or by winning a civil war, to gain control of the Empire.

Pachacutec prophesised many events for humanity and the Earth, which were recorded in the *cutochs,* or knots, in woven tapestries. Much of what was recorded is today becoming a reality.

The prophecies are based on a time line with segments of 500 years known as the *Pachacuti*. *Pachacuti* means to flip time – 'What was is no longer, and what was not now is. At the end of one *Pachacuti* before the beginning of the next is a period of thirty years. This thirty year period is a time of immense change for humanity and the Earth, much like the narrowing of a river, where debris becomes stuck on the river banks and stays behind as the river flows into a wider bed again expanding and free flowing.

We are currently living in one of the thirty year time periods, ending in the year 2012. We then enter into the *tenth Pachacuti* – the next 500 year cycle. 800 years ago when making these prophecies, *Pachacuti* saw an end to the *Inca Empire* – a time of dark depression was how it was described – at the close of the eighth 500 year cycle.

During these thirty year periods there is suffering but calm and transformation is the end result. These cycles express the long journey of human evolution on which we find ourselves.

The era that transpires for humanity from 2012 is called the *Taripaypacha,* an era of immense growth, a time in which, it is prophesised we will arrive at *Ille Tecsi Wiracocha* - God. From 2012 our perception of time and space will start to change. We gradually, over years, enter a new universal cycle with the rest of the universe.

Many Peruvian masters of the Andean Tradition believe that *Pachacutec* will live up to his name and return in 2012. It is believed he will once again 'turn the world' upside down.

Herewith are some of those prophecies, in brackets are possible interpretations of the recorded prophecies, as offered by Kamaq Wageag in his teaching.

We will make huge advances which will enable us to knock on Gods door (**space travel**).

It is prophesised the light will return to the *runas* - human beings (**the light of consciousness**).

We will use the energy of the sun for light in the day and in the night (**solar power**). Houses will become transparent, like the wind (**possibly the use of glass or new building materials**).

Winds will start to change (**influences**); new winds will come from the East, warm winds with strong influences (**global warming or China**).

We will protect ourselves with walls of wind in the future.

The warrior of the North will be brought to his knees, and will collapse completely. (**This can be interpreted as the Northern continents and a breakdown of structures in those places**).

Light, knowledge and wisdom will come from the East, where the sun rises.

Population of the South (**Southern Hemisphere**) who works the land and feed from the Sun will embrace those who live in the Shadows (**areas of the earth will be colder, and will be sustained by the warmer areas / also possibly those who are unconscious**).

Light will become darker (**change in climate**), but the internal light in humans will become brighter (**consciousness**).

We will not need to see with our eyes in the future because we will see with our hearts. This will herald our return to *Ille Tecsi Wiracocha* (***Ille Tecsi Wiracocha* is love and through the activation of the consciousness of the heart centre, we move closer to the Divine**).

In the Andes, produce will be abundant, as will plants and animals. The climate in the Andes will become warmer due to the spirit of the water coming from the depths of the Earth (**this could relate to the cold current in the Pacific Ocean bringing a change in climate in the Andes**).

Humans will need very little clothing in the future for warmth, also very little food for the body to be sustained. The inner sun energy (**Divine fire**) will erase all shadow (**our internal shadow**). The frequency of man becomes very subtle (**energetic vibrations**).

In the eleventh Pachacuti (**1000 years from now**) we will no longer have need of a physical body (**ascension beyond the third dimension**).

It is clear from the above, a future, at least for the next 1000 years, was foreseen for humanity and our continued life on this planet. It is also clear we will go through much climatic and internal change and adaptation, but this is to be expected. Time changes all things in this dimension.

I have heard the masters say many times over the years the feminine will lead the way into the next *Pachacuti*. Many years ago, in one of my meetings with Baba Credo, he told me Africa could only be healed with the feminine energies. This was part of a personal message for me. As a warrior my masculine energy is very powerful, and when Baba Credo spoke these words to me I knew he was referring to the need for me to heal and balance the masculine and feminine aspects of myself, in order to fulfil my life path.

I now understand these statements more generally. Over several years, but especially the last two I have witnessed a rather extraordinary thing take place in human beings. During the one on one channelling sessions, I witnessed the expansion of the feminine energies in woman, and through this a re-ownership of the masculine energy in men. It is as though, while the females have held onto the masculine energy, it was impossible for the males of our species to hold it well and in a healed way.

Women, by owning the masculine and making peace with it within themselves, and men owning their feminine and making peace with it within themselves, essentially are healing the greater wounding between the sexes.

At the appropriate time, the feminine has reactivated, and as it comes into being within the individual, it is held peacefully and gently next to the masculine without threat, fear nor anger. This equalising of the *Yanantin* and *Masantin* (masculine and feminine) within individuals is the most hope filled and beautiful process I have had the privilege to witness.

As this balance is attained within individuals several things begin to happen. We access wholeness within ourselves, not seeking it through relationship to others, or through outside factors. Relationships become inter-dependant and not co-dependent, resulting in healthier interactions, more loving communication. People's expressions become more balanced. With balanced communication our actions and choices better reflect our truth. In the future I believe this will result in social structures being created through balance, and balanced structures will support the individual better than the current ones do.

We still have a long way to go. I see many people in my healing sessions, but the quantity does not even begin to dent world population. I am certain though I am not the only one witnessing this as it is happens all over the world. The seeds planted within us are germinating, but germinating at different rates and different levels of consciousness for different people. It has however, begun - the feminine energies lead the way to healing.

CHAPTER SIXTEEN

THE FIFTH AND THE SIXTH ELEMENT

"This journey brings clarity of self. In the past I linked my identity to groups, but now it is more individualised. I am better able to accept others, the good and bad aspects. I can discern what energies, patterns and issues are mine and which are not, and in a balanced way let go of what is not mine. There is also detachment in that we each must take responsibility for what is ours. I have less self – judgement and derive a sense of joy from being myself. This comes from within; I don't access it from outside of myself. I am gentler and more aware of my environment. I love animals but now feel kindness even for insects, some of which I am afraid of. I realise everything has its role." - Mabel

"I attended the workshop out of curiosity, having received a message from my spiritual guides that I should. I had no idea what it involved or how it would affect me. The information was simple but profound, making perfect sense and made me realise how

disconnected I was from the elements and caught up in the 'rat race' of daily living. It was refreshing and delightful to learn a new way of relating to the elements and the cosmos. The subsequent journey through initiation became a life changing process for me, bringing clarity, purpose and meaning to my life and continuous expansion of consciousness.

My life changes are both internal and external, the external a natural consequence of the internal. For the first time in my life I am in touch with who I really am, what serves me and what does not. I attained peace and harmony. I live my life truthfully and consciously. I am transformed into a person I like and feel good about who I am." - Nela

And so I arrive at the current time. Having completed the *Kuraq Akulleq* initiation I stand deep in its integration process. In my physical world I experienced several difficulties since my return from Peru, some deeply painful, and yet still I stand - firm and true in myself. As these experiences push me from my centre momentarily; my own momentum pulls me back in. I feel the beauty of *Ille Tecsi Wiracocha* resident in me physically. This creates disruption to my bodies frequencies as it adjusts to the change, but its effects are not lasting. I cannot close my heart, I cannot shut down my light – it simply is no longer possible.

It is as if I swam in a pond with many others – going around and around, suddenly to find myself standing on the bank looking at those who continue swimming, realising that constant movement has no purpose. Understanding we humans engage in this until we realize it is no longer necessary, knowing anyone at any time can step from the pond but are so absorbed in that very movement they simply don't – until they do.

Re engaging with the world in the pond, even as I stand separate from it, I still have some challenges, but they are minor. The only thing with lasting value, importance is the dedicated service to humanity and raising consciousness, waking people from the hypnotic movement of their constant swimming so they too can step from the waters of illusion. There is no arrogance in this stance but rather infinite patience and tolerance of the journey. It is what is.

Reaching this place comes after years of journeying. But the journey itself is vital. It is through our balance, our hearts centers expand, connecting our physical bodies to our soul energy. It is through the heart centre that our truth, our spark of Divine Light may be found. It becomes safe to live this spark, expressing it externally to become the living example of Divine truth, ourselves in our purest form. Our external expression becomes loving, powerful and wise. This is the journey to completion and self-mastery.

As we conjugate the four elements and they interact through and within us in balance, we find the skill to manage our feelings, emotions, minds and bodies. As we become adept at this, we master our reactions, reflecting consciously who we are to the external world. Once the heart energy is flowing well, we embrace self-acceptance, it becomes natural to externalize our truth and we become authentic humans. This is the living experience of the fifth element – love.

As authentic humans, we relate to and understand through love our fellow brothers and sisters, our human family, knowing we are the same with a body, a mind and a soul. We all struggle through the physical reality, creating our own dramas, happiness, sadness, fears and hopes. The position in society, the wealth or poverty we experience, the age or generation we are born to, all these things become irrelevant. We are responsible for who we are and what we experience and, together, are the inhabitants, the keepers of this planet Earth, our mother.

This love for our brothers and sisters is an unconditional love, an expression enabling us to give where there is need, for the sake of giving, not analyzing nor judging the recipient. They are human, as we ourselves are, struggling to arrive at their authenticity. This is *Ayni* in action.

Sit silently in front of another human being, a total stranger, and look into their eyes, holding contact with an open heart, feel the love of the ages flow through you and connect to that person. Fear and hatred cannot exist in this state.

This is not love for the sake of fulfillment or satisfaction; it is love simply for the sake of itself, without expectation or need. On this journey I have learnt love is a frequency which does not originate on the Earth plane. It is an expression of soul frequency from the higher realms of Spirit. Through our heart centre we are able to access and express it. Energy flows into our crown centre via the central channel (running parallel to our spine, exiting the body at the root chakra, extending into the earth) as light and as it is externalized at the heart centre is expressed as love, unconditional love, universal love. It does not need reciprocation in this dimension to exist, it is fed from Spirit. As humans, when we are in fear we close our hearts and block the endless flow of love in ourselves. We feel hurt, sad in the absence of love. We create our own wounds through the judgments we make of situations and others, judgments based on our expectations of how things should be, how others should behave. If we choose to keep our hearts open constantly, no matter the circumstances or the behavior of others, we operate through and are present in love.

People actively seek happiness in many ways and in many places, but happiness is right inside us all the time. Through the practice of opening our hearts to our human family we can live it every day of our lives, and our lives will flow in co-operation and grace with the laws of nature.

But this is not the end…

Once the fifth element is activated and functioning within an individual the sixth element activates. It can be described as intuition or intelligent imagination. However, the experience of it is far beyond the meaning of these words. It is not the state of intuition described in previous chapters, as the experience of the psychic senses as channeling and clairaudience. It is an experience of reality in its original energetic state. The access of the sixth element makes this perception possible and brings the ability to influence that reality or change it.

It is an exceptional power to access. I have understood why nature has made the fifth element available before the sixth. When a person is motivated by love, they desire the betterment of the lives of others and the power of the sixth element is not abused.

My access and understanding of the sixth element is a recent one. The first time I became aware of it I was in my home, looking out at the garden. My focus settled on a leaf on the tree closest to me and my perception shifted. Suddenly I saw not only a leaf but its energetic and molecular structures. I was surprised at my perception. I found I could perceive my hands in the same way. I did not alter these structures; it was enough to 'see' them at that stage.

I am now able, through intent alone, to command energies to change. I cannot do this for myself, only for others. Kamaq Wageag says that trying to use ones power for oneself is like a blow torch trying to burn itself. It simply is not possible. So I must do things the old fashioned way for myself – ask Spirit and have gratitude for what I receive.

The visionary journey I underwent in the Auyuscha ceremony was prophetic it seems. I was not only being shown what needed to be cleared to arrive at Ille Tecsi Wiracocha but was shown what was actually going to happen.

The patterns I was shown regarding my relationship with humanity – my worry and concern for others, my desire to protect them - have been made abundantly clear, as has the destructive nature of these patterns, destructive to myself. These patterns translate into self-sacrifice, a consciousness no longer supported by the Universe. Its manifestation, as rescuing, belongs to the age we are moving away from and results in major losses of power.

The energy I stand in now requires that each that enter here walk alone, and like birth or death no one can be carried into this place. And so I continue to love my human brothers and sisters, but I accept the suffering and detours they choose for themselves, and I trust them to arrive when they are ready, even when they do not trust themselves. I no longer need to prove myself or sacrifice myself to prove my worthiness. As I am, I am enough to stand before my Creator in peace.

As we slide into the prophesies and 2012, I am made increasingly aware of the truth of something Pachamama said to me the first time I connected with her, "The world takes its reflections from our own inner perceptions". The more light we bring through us, the more we hold our heart centers open and the more we govern our minds and thoughts, the gentler our transition into the new Universal cycle awaiting us.

AFTER WORD

Over the past twelve years I have become more alive in a way difficult to describe. I feel life with deep abiding consciousness and passion, I know death as an old friend who one day, I will welcome and embrace, I know myself as someone I truly like and have a deep acceptance and love for. I know humanity as my brothers and sisters who walk beside me - each resonating at different frequencies, operating through individualised consciousness, on their own path, all moving towards the same destination. My love for them brings warmth, light and insight to my relationship with them.

I know the Earth to be my mother, supporting, nurturing and holding me as I journey forward, I know the stars to be my real home, and when my heart yearns for something beyond my human understanding, I know the skies will one day embrace me. I know the universe to be my home, the place I belong, and the space where I am limitless and loved. I know *Ille Tecsi Wiracocha* to be my personal and intimate Creator and the light in all the eyes I look into, the smile in all the beauty I encounter and the melody in all songs I hear.

I know above all that I am loved, in this realm and in others, I know through the wholeness and security with which I have been graced my heart centre is the point of beginning and end of all that is, was and will be and I am one with life, love and being. I finally, truly am that I am.

I feel the joy of being alive, the beauty of the currents of love coursing through my veins, my cells, my being responding to this creative force. I know what it is to kneel at the feet of our Creator, to be laid bare of all defences and to be liberated in Divine Presence, to be loved and accepted as I am, in all my humanness. I know what it is to look into the eyes of another human being with this light flowing from my eyes, my presence and watch the light dawn within them, as their lips smile, their eyes light up in recognition of what cannot be explained and is omnipresent. This state of being is humanities destiny in this world, every one.

Such is my journey and the experience with the sacred and ancient Andean Tradition. It is not only my journey; there are others who daily undertake the journey beside me and many more in other parts of the world. This journey has been traversed and mastered by many before me and will be undertaken by many more in generations to come. A journey which has enabled and facilitated my current state of being, and as long as I am, I know this journey will not end. The Divine Will of *Ille Tecsi Wiracocha,* alive inside of me, will lead me where I need to be.

With little time before the next universal cycle is upon us, a time of consciousness and light. We have so much to look forward to in this privileged time in which we live. And look forward is what we should do with our faces turned to the East, to the sun, our shadows behind us, enveloped in the *Pachamama*, as children of the Universe, knowing we are loved, with nothing to fear.

THE INCAS INCORPORATE THE ANDEAN TRADITION

At the height of their reign, the Incas took the best of a culture from a conquered area and incorporated it into the Empire. Thus a number of cultures influenced the Empire, and below are some of the major ones.

THE MOCHE & CHIMU CULTURES

This was a coastal society that existed between 100 and 800A.D.

They left no written records, although possibly records were kept using the *Quipus* technique, an intricate system of knotted coloured threads, used by the Incas. However, it is still to be deciphered. We learn much about them though their ceramics and art. They created monumental architectural structures including the well-known *Tucume* Pyramids. They grew corn, squash, avocado, guavas, chili peppers, and beans. They also domesticated llamas and guinea pigs, and were renowned fishermen and hunters. *Lapis lazuli* and *Spondylus* shell objects made up part of their trade. The *Moche* were expert weavers, gold, silver and copper metallurgists using wax castings and hammered sheet metal.

Purgatorio, purgatory is the name the locals use for the dozens of pre-Hispanic pyramids, enclosures and mounds, making up the site of *Tucume,* covering an area of over 540 acres, encompassing twenty-six major pyramids and platforms.

This was a thriving city of temples and squares built by the *Moche / Si*can in the 11th century, conquered by the *Chimu* in the 14th century, and occupied from 1450 to 1532A.D by the Incas.

Local shaman healers, *curanderos* invoke the power of *Tucume* in their rituals, but locals fear the site. The region's healers, direct descendants of these lost civilizations, are famous throughout Peru for their skill and wisdom.

The tomb of the Lord of *Sipan* in Lambayeque, Peru is the richest burial site discovered in the Western Hemisphere, carbon dated to 290A.D. *Sipan* was a high ranking warrior-priest, named the *Lord of Sipan*. The discovery of the intact tombs of *Sipán* is enormously helpful to Archaeologists in understanding the *Moche* and *Chimu* cultures.

THE HUARI

The *Huari* culture finds prominence in 650A.D, concentrated in the *Lurin Valley* on the central coast of present-day Peru, with influences extending to the central and coastal Andes. They formed part of the *Cuismancu Empire, with* their power centre in

Pachacamac. In Quechua, *Pacha* means world, and *camac* means to animate – The One who animates the World. *Pachacamac* dates back as early as 200B.C, attributed to a culture simply named *early Lima*. The *Huari* expanded on *Pachacamac* constructing architectural compounds but the stepped pyramid, known as the temple of *Pachacamac* is attributed to the preceding culture. The whole construction is aligned with the cardinal points.

Pachacamac is famous as the 'seat of the Oracle', and remained a place of pilgrimage throughout the early Lima and Huari cultures, which is considered one of the most important religious centers of the indigenous peoples of the central Andes.

The *Incas* arrived around 1450A.D, adapting the preexisting temples, adding the *Temple of the Sun*, the *Acllahuasi* (women's temple), the *Palace of Taurichumbi* and the *Seat of the Peregrinos*. The spectacular *Incan Temple of the Sun* is four pyramids overlooking the Pacific Ocean with many of the walls still showing the original red and yellow painted designs.

The *Acllahuasi* is typical Incan architecture, with foundations of polished granite, the living quarters of the *Virgin* priestesses *of the Sun*. This great spiritual center met its demise in 1532 with the Spanish conquest.

THE COLLAGUAS AND CABANAS

Shepherds and herders originally inhabited the *Colca Canyon* region, an area of over 100 km, with an average depth of 3 400 meters from river bed to mountain peak.

Condors nest in the steep cliff-faces around the *Cruz Del Condor*, an area where it is still possible to observe these creatures in their natural habitat. The condor is the heaviest flying bird in the world, weighing up to 12kg, its wingspan in excess of three meters. It is symbolically powerful in the Andean Tradition as the animal totem of the *Hanaq Pacha*, the realms of Spirit.

The *Huari Empire*, from *Ayacucho*, impacted significantly from 600AD to 900AD, incorporating villages from the *Colca* area into its administration. When the *Huari* culture began to disintegrate, local societies separate from the imperial *Wari* administration arose - the *Collagua* in the north and Cabana in the south.

The terraces throughout the canyon indicate the amazing agricultural and architectural skills of the *Collaguas* and *Cabanas*. Agricultural progress is evident in the irrigation of terraced fields through constructed channels using hydraulic technology. Significant because agriculture was the economic resource of the inhabitants of the lower areas, while the higher altitudes supported livestock. Circular domed structures appeared around this time with stone walls cemented with clay.

Around 1450 AD, the *Cabanas* and *Collaguas* were incorporated into the *Incan Empire* by *Inca Tupac Yupanqui*. It is believed this saw barley, quinoa corn, gold and silver brought to the villages strengthening their economy and organization.

THE PARACAS AND NAZCA

This culture flourished from the 1st to the 8th centuries AD along the dry Southern coastline of Peru, the River Valley of the *Rio Grande De Nazca* and the *Ica Valley*. It was greatly influenced by the *Paracas* culture which produced complex textiles and crafts from various materials including *spondylus* shell, pottery and small amounts of gold and silver. They were also well known for their brain surgery and cranial trepanation.

A site of natural hills at *Cahuachi,* in the lower portion of the *Nazca* valley seems to have been established during the late *Paracas* culture, and was further modified, by the *Nazca* people into pyramid mounds. This ceremonial site was abandoned mid-way through the *Nazca* civilization, possibly due to drought brought about by de-forestation. Because of the extreme environment, their spiritual beliefs and practices were centred on agriculture and fertility, and deities took the form of animals and fish. They used hallucinogenic plants, *San Pedro* cactus, to induce visioning.

The *Nazca* were known as the "sand painters" because of the famous *Nazca* lines, by the removal of rocks and stones over vast areas, creating perfect pictures of animals and birds called Geoglyphs. During the same time frame they mastered their environment, successfully extracting water for irrigation, improving crops, extending cultivated areas, and building terraced pyramids.

In about 500A.D, a major El Niño built up in the Pacific, deluging the Andes with rain, resulting in water walls washing down the valleys, sweeping away the crops, buildings and artifacts in its path.

After this, the *Nazca* civilization became fragmented and fought among themselves. At this time the *Huari* people came down from the nearby mountains, conquering the remnants of the Nazca, incorporating them into *Huari* society, who in turn fell to the *Inca* in 1450A.D.

THE LUPACA, UROS AND PEOPLE OF LAKE TITIKAKA

Petro glyphs and paintings show evidence the *Lupaca* and *Colla* tribe date back about 8 000 years, although structures in the Lake *Umayo* area date to 1000A.D. The burial towers at *Cutimbo* are an example of this, with large round stone towers, *Chullpas*, dotting the landscape. At *Sillustani complex* the *Chullpas* were built to house remains of local *Colla* tribe leaders (1200 - 1450A.D) called *Hatuncolla* in the northern lake area. *Chullpa* sites are also found on the South Western Shores of Lake Titicaca.

The *Uros* people inhabit the floating Islands on the *Puno* bay of Lake Titicaca, the islands and the dwellings are built entirely of *Totora* reeds. They speak the *Uru* language and predate the *Incas*.

The *Amantaní Island,* Lake Titicaca, covers nearly nine square kilometers and is characterized by its natural fauna, including *La muña* – used for altitude sickness and *Kantuta,* Peru's national flower. Eight communities live on the island, cultivating potatoes, corn, coca, quinoa, and beans. This island is home to the *Pachatata* and *Pachamama temples.*

TIWANAKU

Tiawanaku in Bolivia lies off the South Eastern shore of Lake Titicaca and it's believed the name originates from the Aymara language – *taypiqala* - meaning 'stone in the center'. However, *Tiawanaku's people* had no written language. Between 300A.D. and 1000A.D, the *Tiawanaku* flourished from a small agricultural village into a cosmological center.

Agriculturally rich, with a social hierarchy, using politics to structure its colonies and negotiate trade agreements, they were a predatory people, conquering other tribes and expanding their influence into Bolivia, Peru and Chile.

The community grew enormously between 600A.D. and 800A.D. becoming an important power in the southern Andes. Recent satellite imaging maps of the area of the three primary *Tiawanaku* valleys indicate possible population of between 285,000 and 1,482,000 people.

Tiawanaku gained much power through trade implemented between all the cities within its empire. The ruling hierarchy gained status by controlling surplus food, particularly llama herds, thus controlling transportation within the Empire.

Around 950 A.D. rainfall dropped significantly in the *Titicaca* area, and with it food production. As surplus food decreased, the ruling class began losing power. By 1000A.D. the Empire's source of power and authority dried up and land was uninhabited for many years, except in isolated area by remnants of the *Tiawanaku* people.

In 1445, *Pachacuti Inca Yuipanqui*, the ninth Inca began conquering the *Titicaca* regions. He incorporated the remnants of the *Tiawanaku* culture, and *Quechua* became the official language. *Viracocha*, a man-god worshipped by the *Tiawanaku,* shaper and destroyer of worlds, was replaced by *Inti* and *Ille Tecsi Wiracocha.*

GLOSSARY

Allpa or Allpamama – the Earth Element, literally Earth

Apu – mountain Spirit or consciousness of the mountains

Aumata – Andean Priest (male or female)

Ayni – the Andean system or law of reciprocity

Ayllu Alto Misayoq – first stage of third level initiation, beginning of mastery

Chakana – the Andean cross of balance

Despacho – the ceremony of gratitude performed through an element to the Creator for the community

Hanaq Pacha – the upper world, realms of Spirit or the dimensions of the super conscious

Hucha – heavy dense energy

Illapa – lightning, also referring to energy at the base of the spine which travels up the spine as we evolve, same as Kundalini energy

Ille Tecsi Wiracocha – meaning the one with no name and is the name for the

Inti – the Spirit or consciousness of the Sun

Inti Raymi – sun rise ceremony performed on the winter solstice

Kay Pacha – the physical material world in which we live

Kuraq Akulleq – fourth level initiation, Master of the Coca

Llagte Alto Misayoq – second stage of third level initiation

Llankay – the Andean principle labour and productivity

Malku Inka – sixth level Initiation – Presently unavailable to humanity but prophesised for the future

Mama Kia – the Spirit or consciousness of the Moon

Mama Oclla – wife to Manco Capac and the female part of the legendary couple sent by Inti to help humanity

Manco Capac – the legendary first Inka who rose from the waters of Lake Titicaca and founded the Inkan empire

Masantin – masculine energy

Mesa – the 'power bundle' of the Andean priest

Munay – the Andean principle of unconditional love

Nawis – energy centres on the body, same as 'chakras'

Nina – the Fire

Nogan Kani Kani – the divine presence of 'I am that I am'

Pacha Camac – the great Spirit or consciousness that lives in all that exists

Pachamama – Mother Nature

Pampa Misayoq – the second level of initiation, the first stage of priesthood

Paqo – the first level of initiation, the spiritual seeker

Sacha mama – the 'mother of the waters', the guardian of the sub conscious

Sami – light energy

Sangoma – African Shaman or Medicine man

Sapa Inka – fifth level initiation, presently unavailable to humanity but prophesised by 2012

Suyu – an area, corner or village

Suyu Llagte Alto Misayoq – third and last stage of third level

Tawantinsuyo – the four corners of the Inkan Empire

Taytanchis – the seventh and final level of initiation for humanity

Uju Pacha – the underworld, the realm that exists inside the Earth or dimension of the sub conscious

Unu mama - the water

Wirajoya – herb from Peru burnt as incense, nicknamed 'the internet'

Wyra – the Wind

Yanantin – feminine energy

Yanchay – the Andean principle of Wisdom

Zingar – the ritual of sniffing liquid tobacco in preparation of ingesting San Pedro

Published by Graysonian Press 2012

www.graysonian.com

pat@graysonian.com

+27 11 4311274 (South Africa)

0450260348 (Australia)

For a catalogue of our "inspirational books that change the world" use the above contact details.

Contact the Author

www.sallyrossiter.co.za

marsal@global.co.za

www.ingramcontent.com/pod-product-compliance
Lightning Source LLC
Chambersburg PA
CBHW072002290426
44109CB00018B/2106